BEHAVE YOURSELF, BETHANY BRANT

PATRICIA BEATTY

William Morrow and Company, Inc. / New York

For my young neighbors and manuscript evaluators:
Betty Salley
Mary Salley
Elizabeth MacLaughlin

Library of Congress Cataloging-in-Publication Data
Beatty, Patricia, 1922-
Behave yourself, Bethany Brant.
SUMMARY: A preacher's daughter with lots of curiosity
and a penchant for getting into trouble has an eventful
year and a half, as all the predictions of a fortune-
teller at a Texas county fair in 1898 come true.
[1. Clergymen's families — Fiction. 2. Texas —
Fiction] I. Title.
PZ7.B380544Be 1986   [Fic]   86-12517
ISBN 0-688-05923-6

CONTENTS

⊷ I ⊷

THE
FIRST THING

I'm Bethany Clarinda Brant, a preacher's daughter.

People seem to think being a minister's girl is a mighty fine thing—better than being a teacher's or blacksmith's kid. They think all we ever see is sweetness and light. In my house that was true most of the time because Pa and Mama didn't fight and were as good in their hearts as a minister and his wife were supposed to be. But that doesn't mean that a preacher's daughter gets all her goodness just by catching it from them.

In my case, that is especially true. I am not naturally as good as Pa is. In fact, there's a tiny part of me that church folks might call just plain wicked. Oh, I always knew because I was a preacher's offspring that I was expected to be more holy than most kids my age. Most of the time I try hard to be—but not always.

You see, there is this curiosity bump on my head. The head-bump feeler had told me about it two years ago, when I was nine. It was a big bump—so big that he'd said, "Remember, little girl, it was curiosity that killed the cat." Everybody who'd heard him laughed while my face turned red.

And on that hot day in August 1898, my head bump was itching mightily as I wandered by myself around the county fairgrounds, circling that odd, wicked-looking tent. After going to four Texas county fairs in a row I could honestly say that I had never set eyes on a tent like that anywhere. It was little and it had purple stripes on one side, red on another, and green and blue on the other two. Out front was a yellow and black sign that read:

QUEEN FAREETA KNOWS ALL
FIVE CENTS TO HEAR ALL

The second "all" was in red paint.

Who was Queen Fareeta? And what did she know?

Pa had given me fifteen cents to spend at the fair, which was held at the county seat. I'd spent five cents eating barbecue with my brother, Abel, while Pa and Mama were away at the bandstand listening to the music. Mama was musical and played the organ at our church in Blue Fork, Texas.

Just before he left me and my little brother, who was nine, Pa had smiled and said half jokingly what he always did when he left us, "Behave yourselves, you two. Remember who you are and what you are."

After hearing that, Abel decided that the best way for us to behave ourselves was to split up. Pa and Mama would be busy being musical for at least an hour, and since I wanted to see the quilt exhibit and my brother wanted to view the biggest hog in the county, I thought his idea was a good one. We agreed to come back at three o'clock and eat more barbecue at the pit. He wasn't one bit interested in fancy work, and I wasn't interested in hogs, no matter how big.

It was after I saw the quilts and the knit and crocheted things and the yards of hand-tatted lace in the big fancy work shed that I spotted that striped tent hidden behind it.

Should I go inside and see what "knows all" meant? Did I dare to? My curiosity had me by the throat. I just had to find out what Queen Fareeta knew.

I looked around me real quick. Nobody else was around, so I scooted inside, my heart thumping. There was a dark, heavyset lady all duded up in lots of scarves and strings of beads sitting at a little table.

Noticing that she didn't wear a crown, I asked her, "Are you Queen Fareeta?"

She answered in a deep voice. "I am Fareeta, yes. Curly

top, I know your past, present, and your future."

This surprised me and I said, "How can you know those things when you don't even know me?"

"Sit down, princess with the golden hair, and you will find out for five cents."

I sat down and gave her five pennies. She picked up a deck of cards, shuffled them, and frowned. Cards! I drew back and stood up. Pa was dead set against cards. He said they were the "devil's prayer book." I started to get up.

Queen Fareeta saw my face and laughed. "Sit down. No, we ain't going to play card games, honey. You cut 'em for me. That's all you have to do. I lay 'em out."

Well, so long as I wasn't going to play, I guessed it would be all right. I cut the cards and, fast as a jackrabbit, she spread them out on the table. Bending over them like a buzzard, she told me, "You will be moving soon. There's some bad ahead for you, and some good, too. Your pa's a preacher, huh?"

I let out a gasp. Frog warts! She'd hit that nail right on the head. How did she know?

She grinned with a mouth full of gold teeth. "Right, wasn't I, blue eyes? Well, as I say, there's plenty ahead for you. Now, let's see what the water tells us." She hauled a glass pitcher filled with water out from under her table and set it next to the cards.

I said, "If it says I'm thirsty, I'm not."

"This ain't for drinking. It can show me pictures—if it wants to."

I asked, "Can I see 'em on my side of the pitcher?"

"It ain't likely you can. It takes years of practice to see things."

Queen Fareeta stared at the pitcher and I did, too, but I couldn't see even a bubble. Suddenly she cried, "I see a one-eyed man. He will befriend you when you need him most."

"I don't know any one-eyed men."

She waved her hand at me as if she were shooing away one of the flies in her tent. "He's in your future." She was quiet for a little bit after that, then went on to say, "There will be elephants for you, too!"

Elephants? I clapped my hands over my mouth to keep from laughing at her and her old pitcher. The only elephant I'd ever seen was in a book at our school in Blue Fork. Elephants in Texas? Ha!

Queen Fareeta was vexed with me now. She told me, "I *saw* elephants. They're hard to miss. They're big and they're gray. I know one when I see one, anywhere I see it."

Figuring there would be more one-eyed men in Texas than elephants, I wanted to know more about him. "What'd the one-eyed galoot look like?" I said.

"I didn't see him. That came to me in words in the water—'one-eyed man, friend in need.' "

I asked, "Is that all? Do you do anything else now?"

"No. What do you want for five cents? You got cards and pictures, and that's all."

I reckoned she thought I was rude, and I was sorry for laughing—but *elephants*!

I felt guilty and more wicked than I'd ever felt before. Now I wished I hadn't let my curiosity bump get the best of me. I didn't like hearing what Queen Fareeta knew, after all. Why had I gone inside her old tent? Pa said God saw everything looking down from heaven. I was sure he wouldn't take to what Queen Fareeta did for a living or what I'd done in giving her my pennies. Would God punish me?

I got up, thanked her politely no matter what, and left. As I walked around the fairgrounds I asked myself how she had ever guessed I was a preacher's daughter. It must have been because of the way I reacted to her cards. Queen Fareeta was a smart old bird.

Thinking about that one-eyed man and the bad coming my way made me shiver in spite of the heat, but when I thought of her elephants, I had to laugh again. That was purely loco of her. She must be a big old liar. That's what she was!

One thing for sure—I could never tell Pa and Mama about my going into her tent. She was a fortune-teller, and Pa didn't hold with them any more than he did with cards. But I'd sure remember what I'd given up five cents for. It wasn't just bad, it had been wasteful.

It had started to rain when I'd left the tent, and it was storming worse when Abel, Mama, Pa, and I started for home in our wagon. Abel and I got up fast and sat on the backseat behind Mama, who was fanning herself with her hat. I saw her face as a big, wide streak of lightning lit up the dark gray sky. She was pale, paler than I'd ever seen her look. She didn't look one bit well.

Before I could ask her what was wrong, another awful clap of thunder came, and our team nickered and pulled in their traces. By now the summer storm was directly over the fairgrounds.

It lasted only a few minutes, and when it was quiet again, except for the pittering of hot rain, Pa said, laughing, "Just smell the brimstone in the air. It isn't just the storm. I'd say there's some devilment hereabouts. Have you two behaved yourselves while your mother and I were gone?"

"Yes, Pa," said Abel.

Pa's eyes turned to me and I told a lie. "Oh, yes, I was good."

"What did you do, Bethany?"

"I went to see the quilts and the fancy work after I ate, and then I ate some more." Feeling guilty about Queen Fareeta, I lied again. The thunder rumbling made me think of God getting mad at me.

Next Pa turned to Mama and asked, "How do you feel now, Dulcie?"

She told him softly, "Not so good, Nat. We shouldn't have come to the fair in this heat. It was too much for me, I'm afraid. I should have stayed home, even though I would have missed the beautiful music."

When we got home, Mama lay down right away on the parlor couch.

Pa ordered me, "Go up and change your clothes, Bethany. You get supper tonight."

"Pa, it won't be as good as Mama's cooking."

"That doesn't matter. Supper don't have to be fancy. I'll start the fire in the kitchen stove for you."

I went up to my room, took off my pale blue muslin dress, and hung it up to let the rain spots on it dry. Then I took off my white slippers and set them beside the bed. After putting on my old blue gingham and high-topped shoes, I came downstairs. I'd been hoping Mama would be up by now, but she wasn't. She was lying on our gray velvet sofa with her eyes tightly closed.

I came into the kitchen where the fire was crackling in the stove and saw Pa and Abel sitting at the table. Both of them looked down in the mouth.

I asked, "What's wrong?"

Pa answered, "It's your mama, Bethany. Abel's just about to go for the doctor."

"What's she got, Pa, the fever and red spots Abel had last week?"

"No. Abel, you know where Dr. Griffith lives?"

"Sure, Pa," Abel replied, and ran out the back door with his shirttails flapping.

Pa told me softly, "Bethany, you're old enough to know, and we may be needing your help more than usual, so I'm going to tell you. Your mother's going to give you and Abel a new baby brother or sister around the first of the year."

I was pleased to hear this and immediately hoped for a baby sister. "Oh, that'd be just fine."

"I think so, too. Things aren't going too good for your mother this time, though. She gets weary faster than she did when you and your brother were on the way. She felt poorly at the fair and told me she's felt that way pretty often lately though she never said so till today. Will you make a cup of tea to take in to her?"

"Sure, I will. Do you want Abel to know about the new baby, too?"

Now Pa grinned at me. Nathaniel Brant, my father, was a handsome, yellow-headed man with teeth as white as a wolf's. Abel resembled him. He told me, "If you want to tell Abel, go ahead. Your mama may be resting a lot from now on. It'd be good if you and your brother would be quieter around here, so Abel ought to know why he has to be."

I came closer and asked, "Will Mama be all right?"

"I figure she will. I'm going in now to sit and read to her before supper."

After my father left, I stood awhile beside the table thinking. Mama had been teaching me to cook and do most everything else womenfolk could around a kitchen. Yes, I'd help her wherever I could.

While I peeled the potatoes I worried, though. I recalled what Queen Fareeta had said about there being something "bad" ahead for me. Even if I didn't put any faith in elephants and one-eyed men, I had to admit that some badness had already come true. And it had come true mighty fast—even before we were out of the fairgrounds. I just hoped that was all the badness there would be and that God would overlook what I'd done.

Except for Mama's feeling poorly, the rest of the summer went by like the one we had the year before—hot as blue blazes. You could tell Mama felt the heat by the slow way she went around the house. She was quiet, too, and pale and sick to her stomach in the mornings. She didn't complain, though, and still played the organ at church every Sunday morning, though she gave up visiting sick folks in town.

I started the fifth grade in the fall, so I couldn't be home with Mama all day long anymore. When school started in September, Pa got Mrs. Tompkins, a church widow lady, to come in days to be with Mama. She was a small, plump-bodied, gray-headed lady with quick-moving hands. Her voice carried when she talked. I knew her as long as I could remember.

One day in the middle of November, the day of the first snow, I heard Mrs. Tompkins talking at the back door with another church lady. "Missus Brant's gettin' more peaked and pinched in the face by the day. The preacher and his young'uns don't seem to notice it, though."

Mrs. Tompkins was wrong. I had noticed it. After she

went upstairs to my parents' bedroom with an armload of blankets to keep Mama warmer in bed, I walked over to one of the two parlor windows to watch the snow falling so quietly on the street that nobody could hear it. Already it had covered up the flowering plants along our front walk. I had watered them faithfully all summer long to keep them alive because Mama loved them so. She'd planted them in the spring. It gave her pleasure to sit in the parlor with the portieres pulled back and admire them, but now there wasn't anything of them to see there but cold white snow.

It snowed and thawed and then froze up and snowed again all winter long. All we saw was bare ground and whiteness, and after a while it got to be a tiresome sight. I never fancied winter, and this year I hated it even more with Mama getting no better. I missed going over to visit my schoolmates after school and on Saturdays; but, after all, I was the girl of the house and the oldest child, and it mostly fell on me to help out. I could have grumbled to Pa, but I didn't. I could tell by the look on his face sometimes that he was worried about Mama. And so was I.

November ended and December arrived. By the middle of the month, Mama had quit playing the organ and was in bed all the time, being looked after hand and foot. She'd lie there quietly, her long black hair in one big braid to keep it from snarling. She'd smile at me but rarely said anything. Mama had never been much of a chatterer. There was a quietness deep inside her that was natural to her.

On Christmas Eve, though, after telling me how to make

11

raisin sauce for the Christmas ham, she reached for my hand and said, "I wish I could fix up a good Christmas for you and Abel, honey, but I can't—not this year. You're a credit to your papa and me, Bethany. You do well at school. Keep on doing that. Keep Abel at his studies, too. You'll grow up to be a fine woman. I'm proud of you and of Abel, too. Tell him that. He'd be flustered if I did. I hear he knows all about the new baby coming."

"I told him and he's tickled about it. We want to know what you'll call it."

"We haven't settled on any names yet, but it will be something from the Bible, of course, like you and Abel. He's named after a person. You're named after a town in the Holy Land. There are a couple of names in my head. Bethany, I want to talk to you about your father."

"What about him, Mama?"

"He needs a lot of looking after. Most men think they don't, but they do. Mrs. Tompkins says you're very helpful to her. I'm glad you've looked after Pa and Abel so well since I've been down."

"I've tried to, Mama."

She let go of my hand now and turned her pale face away. Then she said, "Once the baby's come, it may take some time for me to get my strength back, so I'll still be needing you to lean on."

"That's all right. Can I fetch you anything—a cup of tea? The doctor's wife sent over a new book for you, one of Robert Louis Stevenson's."

"Thank you, honey, but I don't feel like reading right now. Maybe tomorrow I will, though."

That was the last time I got to talk alone with Mama. After Christmas Day Dr. Griffith came to our house every single day. By the end of the year there was a nurse with Mama almost all the time, and she kept Abel and me out of her room.

A couple of days into 1899, on a snowy Saturday morning, the baby started to come. Dr. Griffith came right away and ordered Abel and me over to Mrs. Tompkins's house on the outskirts of town.

Abel and I waited all night long in Mrs. Tompkins's little parlor. We talked about lots of things, trying to comfort each other, but it didn't work. We looked at stereopticon slides of the Pacific Northwest, but couldn't even keep our minds on the big trees we saw. Eventually we tried to sleep but didn't get much rest. We were both too worried about Mama.

Pa came early Sunday morning. It was one of those rose-colored dawns that come up over snow, the kind that makes the whole world look pink. Pink made me think of girls, and I wondered if we had a baby sister.

Mrs. Tompkins was still upstairs in bed, so I opened the door for Pa. The sun was at his back and I couldn't see his face. He didn't say anything. Neither did I. Suddenly I felt that I had a big boulder on my chest. I *knew*!

Abel, who stood behind me, cried out, "Is the baby here, Pa?"

13

"He's here, Abel." Pa's voice was deep and soft.

"He's a boy, huh?" My brother's happy voice trailed off. He knew something was wrong, too.

"Yes, he came. Tell Mrs. Tompkins you two are to stay here today with her."

"Why, Pa?" I asked, "why can't we come home?"

Pa didn't speak for a long time, then he said, "They're gone, both of 'em, the baby and your mother."

"Where'd they go?" cried Abel, pushing at my arm as I held him back.

"God's will, it was God's will." Pa turned around and walked away. I watched him for a bit, then shut the door.

"Gone?" said my brother, staring at me.

I knew what Pa had meant. I couldn't move. I couldn't grab hold of Abel to hold him.

He kept at me, though, and finally I told him, "Abel, they're dead. Both of 'em died. Mama wasn't strong enough for herself or for him to live. We have to stay here till Pa sends for us."

"But I want to go home now!"

"So do I, but we mustn't. I'll go up and tell Mrs. Tompkins."

As I raised my fist to rap at Mrs. Tompkins's door, a flood of cold rose up out of my midsection and settled around my heart.

"Oh, Mama!" my heart cried out, but no words came to my lips as Mrs. Tompkins, in her flannel nightgown, opened the door.

14

My face told her the news. She sighed, shook her head, and cried, "Oh, my dear, oh, my dear girl, my dear little girl."

I found my voice to say, "My brother's little yet—I ain't. I'm eleven."

I went down to Abel, who had buried his face in a sofa pillow. His shoulders were shaking, and I sat down beside him and laid my cheek to his back. That was how we sat until Mrs. Tompkins came down to lay the fire.

I wished I could cry the way she and Abel did, but I couldn't.

꧁ 2 ꧂

THE
SECOND THING!

The next morning the sound of a distant explosion woke me up. I knew what that was. It was dynamite. I had heard it before, last winter, when so many folks in town had died of la grippe. The ground was ice-cold hard, and they had had to dynamite a place in the cemetery for Mama and my little baby brother. The sound was like a fist in my head.

Mrs. Tompkins had rousted out black duds for us to wear at the funeral, and afterward, for six months' time. We dressed quickly and arrived home that morning to find our house full of folks from the church and others I'd never set eyes on before. They had come through roads dug in the snow to be with us today.

At noon it started to snow some more. The funeral was at the graveyard, not the church. Abel and I watched as the burying box was lowered with ropes and dirt was thrown on top if it. I'd brushed the snow off of one of Mama's peony plants, pulled it up, and brought it with me. It was sort of greeny-black in January, but I threw it on top of the coffin, anyway, because I knew it would have pleased Mama. Nobody had brought flowers; there weren't any this time of the year.

Although Pa usually preached at the funerals at our church, he didn't at Mama and the baby's. A preacher from the next town did. With him was a big, white-haired fat man who had been visiting him when Mama died. This white-haired man was the bishop of Pa's district and was the most important minister in our part of the state.

The bishop stood beside the other preacher while he talked about Mama's goodness and kindness and her right to go to heaven. Lots of ladies cried into their handkerchiefs, and men, with their hats off out of respect, blew their noses quite a bit. Abel sniffled beside me and Pa, but I just couldn't cry. My heart felt stepped on. My eyes burned like fire the way my chest did, but there weren't any tears. I pulled down my hat to cover my face as best as I could and brought my neck scarf up as far as it went so folks wouldn't see me not crying. Let them think I was covered up to keep off the freezing wind that blew from the north.

I thought about Mama, seeing in my head what I remembered about her. I saw her sitting in her Sunday best at the church organ with her long fingers moving over the keys. How straight her back always was! Her hair gleamed black under her wide-brimmed gray Sunday hat with the dark blue ribbons and little white plumes. Sometimes the church folks didn't sing while she played. Instead we'd all just listen as she played beautiful solo pieces, then hymns or other sacred music from the great composers.

I thought about her, too, being busy in the kitchen making mince pies for the holidays, rolling out the crust so tender and flaky that eating it was like eating cookies. I remembered her crocheting antimacassars for our sofa and chairs, knitting warm mittens for Abel and me, and tatting lace to trim her and my petticoat hems. Mama's hands were always moving.

Mama had loved animals—not the big ones like horses and cows, but birds and puppies and kittens. Folks from the church brought her newborn kittens and puppies they couldn't keep, and Mama always found good homes for them with other church folks or with kids from our school. When our old dog had died last year, she couldn't bear to get another one right away, so we didn't have one at all now.

Oh, I loved her so much and missed her so terribly. Why couldn't I cry for her?

Finally the funeral was over and everyone climbed into wagons and came back to our house to eat all the food the church ladies had brought. Because I knew folks were watching me and expecting me to eat, I dabbed at my plate. Then I went upstairs and threw myself across my bed, wanting to cry. Crying had never come easy to me the way it did to other girls at school, even when I cut or burned myself or stubbed my toe.

The tears were behind my eyes, but I just couldn't get them out. "Mama, Mama," I whispered over and over to myself, knowing that my life would never be the same again.

And it wasn't. Mrs. Tompkins came in to cook and clean while I was at school. Church ladies brought over covered suppers and invited us to their houses for dinner.

Everything in the house reminded me of Mama, even the pots and the pans. Abel told me he felt the same way. We could tell how Pa felt because he stayed in his office at the church as much as he could, no matter how cold it was there. The deacons and the other men in the church visited with him in his office, and the bishop came in on the railroad to see him in March. The two of them talked a long, long time in our parlor, with the doors closed. From the kitchen I didn't hear one word.

The next night, though, Pa told us what he and the bishop had discussed. As we sat after supper with our kerosene lamp smoking because I'd forgotten to trim the wick, Pa opened up to Abel and me. "Bethany and Abel," he began, "I've got something to say to you. We'll all be moving away from here next month. I talked with the bishop yesterday. He knows how I feel about living here in Blue Fork now that your mother's gone. It's like I expect to see her everywhere all the time. I can't keep my mind on things the way I ought to and do the Lord's work for others here anymore. After your mama died, I started writing back and forth to her only brother, Uncle Luke Morris. You remember him and his family, don't you? Anyway, I wrote him about how things are here now. He wrote me back last week and asked us to come out West and live on his ranch outside of Prineville, Texas."

"But we won't have a house of our own anymore!" I protested.

"No, not for a while at least. Prineville's a hundred or so miles west of here in cattle country that's just opening up to settlers. Your uncle's family was just about the first folks out there. There isn't a church there yet, but Uncle Luke says there'll surely be one before long because townfolk want one and are willing to collect money for it and a house for a pastor."

Abel asked, "Where'll you preach, Pa?"

"In the town in stores and lodge halls—wherever I can." He stopped, then went on. "The bishop said the Lord could use me there as a circuit rider till there's a new church. He's already arranged it with the bishop of that district."

I sucked in my breath. I knew what that meant, and I didn't like it. Mama had once told me that when she and Pa had first gotten married, he had been a circuit-riding minister until he got the Blue Fork church. He'd ridden hundreds and hundreds of miles on horseback from town to town and farm to farm to preach, marry folks, and bury

20

them properly. Mama'd said that she had been alone weeks and weeks on end. Being a circuit rider at Pa's age meant he was sort of starting all over again.

I said, "Pa, you'd be leaving us all alone a lot."

"No, Bethany, not alone. You'll be with Luke, his wife, Reva, and Mattywill, his girl, and the new baby, Billy Bob."

"Billy Bob, a baby boy?" Abel interrupted.

"Yes, Abel, he'd be about the same age as . . ." Pa's voice trailed off as he got up to go to the stove and pour himself some more of my greenish-colored coffee. I was a bad coffee maker. I never roasted the beans in the oven the way Mama did.

Abel and I knew that Pa was hurting inside the way we were, but how could we help him?

When he sat back down, he told me, "Bethany, because of the new baby, Aunt Reva could use help around the house more than Mattywill gives her. And, Abel, Luke could use you on the ranch."

"Has he got horses?" Abel wanted to know.

"You bet. And cowboys, too. Mostly he raises cattle."

"When'll we leave?" I asked.

"The middle of next month. That's when the new preacher'll be coming here to Blue Fork to take over for me. I'll tell Mrs. Tompkins the news of our leaving tomorrow."

I had another question for him. "What about our furniture, Pa?"

"It'll be stored in a warehouse here till I send for it. It

can be sent to us by railroad after there's a manse for us."

Abel asked, "Will we have to go to school if we live on a ranch?"

This made Pa grin. "Of course. Luke wrote that Mattywill, who's about your age, Bethany, will be starting school. The schoolhouse that's being built will be furnished by fall. She'll ride a horse to school. So will the two of you."

I whispered the wonderful word—*horse*. I'd ridden a horse but never had a saddle horse of my own. Nobody who lived in town needed one here in Blue Fork. I thought about this all the while I washed the supper dishes later that evening. It wasn't until I was all through with my chores that something that had caught in the back of my mind popped out. Queen Fareeta! She had told me that I'd *move*. The second of her predictions had come true!

Although I wasn't overjoyed about moving, there could be some good at that. There was Mattywill, my cousin. She was a girl my age, and I'd always wanted a sister. I'd heard of Mattywill all my life but had never set eyes on her. Now I began to wonder what she'd be like.

The cold spring days went by slowly as Pa arranged for us to leave. Our furniture would be put in storage after we left, and Mrs. Tompkins would clean the house for the new minister who was coming from Fort Worth.

I was packing linens in a bureau for storage when we got the last storm of the year, a blue norther coming down from

Canada. It hit full force in the middle of the night. I heard it in bed and shivered at the sound of the wind and sleet outside, ducking my head under the warm quilts. The next morning when I got up to see how much snow we'd gotten, I found a little gray-and-brown bird dead on my windowsill. The norther had caught the birds that had just come in from wintering in the south by surprise.

I took the bird inside and held its stiff, icy-cold body in my hand. As I looked down at it something busted open inside me and I started to cry. It was strange that I could cry for a frozen-to-death bird when I couldn't cry for Mama and the baby. I didn't go to school that day. Everybody let me be, and I cried all day long. By dark I was all cried out.

In my mind it seemed to me that I was ready to leave for Prineville. Now that I'd cried for my mother and little brother, I wouldn't be leaving a part of me behind here in Blue Fork.

Our last night in Blue Fork, the church ladies had a farewell supper for us. I could tell they liked us and hated to see us leave, but they understood why. They gave us presents, too—a Bible in a waterproof metal box for Pa to take on his circuit rounds, and new school slates for Abel and me. They even packed a big picnic basket of food for us to eat on the train because they were afraid that the food at the cafés along the way might be awful. One by one they hugged us and promised to put flowers on Mama's and the baby's graves every week.

23

We were at the depot with our valises early the next morning, waiting for the westbound train. As we sat on the platform bench, I asked Pa, "Will Uncle Luke meet us in Prineville?"

"I think so. His ranch is ten miles out of town. I wrote him when our train pulls in."

"Do you suppose Mattywill will be with him?"

"Maybe so. Are you looking forward to meeting her?"

I nodded. I surely was. There were other female cousins on Pa's side of the family, but they were grown-up and married. Mattywill Morris was the only girl cousin my age. I hoped we'd be best friends.

Once upon a time I'd thought I'd like riding on a train, but after the first day on this one I changed my mind. The aisles were dirty, and the little black stove at the end of the car let out smoke. Our seats were as hard as fence posts. The noises the train made were loud, and the engine's whistle made me jump every time I heard it. The sleeping cars were full by the time the train got to Blue Fork, so we had to sit up all night long. Abel curled up and slept, but not Pa and me. We talked about President McKinley and Texas Rangers and things like that—not about what we'd left behind in Blue Fork. The food the church ladies had given us became stale, so I opened up a window and threw it out. The coyotes I'd seen now and then on the prairie would get it. They were always hungry.

We pulled into Prineville around noon two days after we'd left Blue Fork. Pa had told us that it was at a junction between two railroads, and settlers were pouring in for farmland. I gave Prineville a good going-over from the train window. All I could say about it was that it appeared to be on its way to becoming a town but hadn't quite gotten there yet. Lots of it wasn't finished. I could look right through some buildings that didn't have any siding nailed up yet. Others were up but had no paint on them. Even over the clackety noise of our train I could hear the sounds of hammers busily at work.

Pa leaned forward across Abel to tell me, "There aren't many trees fit for lumber around here. This is prairie country. Luke said that the lumber is hauled in on the railroad and down the river."

Abel wanted to know, "Is it a good fishing river?"

"Maybe so. You'll have to ask your Uncle Luke. There may be catfish."

"Can you cook a catfish?" Abel asked me.

The question made me snort. "There's nothin' at all to frying up a fish." I asked Pa, "Which one of the buildings out there is the new schoolhouse?"

He peered around, then shook his head. "Bless me if I know. All buildings look alike when they're just tall boards sticking up. It takes awhile to know what it'll be or to judge its size without the siding. Come on, the train's stopped. Let's get off."

25

Uncle Luke wasn't there as we had expected. Other folks got out of their cars and left the station right away, but not us Brants. In a few minutes there wasn't anybody at all on the platform except us and a yellow dog. He sat there, stared at us, then got up and ran down the side steps to the ground.

Pa and Abel and I sat on the bench in the sun and waited there for an hour by Pa's pocket watch. He was about to get up and talk to the stationmaster when a boy came riding up to the platform on a black-and-white horse. He jumped off and came clomping up the steps.

He was a mite taller than I was, with dark hair, dog-brown eyes, and a dark complexion. He wore a big brown felt hat, a neck bandanna, a shirt and vest, striped pants, and big dusty boots. He asked Pa, "Are you the preacher Brant from Blue Fork?" His voice was high.

"Yes, I am. Who'd you be, son?"

"Howdy." The boy stuck out his hand and shook hands with Pa, then with me and Abel. After that he said, "I'd be Mattywill Morris, kin to you." Off came the hat to let long, almost black hair fall onto the shoulders of the fringed leather vest.

I could see that Pa was trying to hide his surprise as he said, "These are your cousins, Bethany and Abel."

But I gawked. This was Mattywill? This boyish-looking girl was my cousin?

Abel was even blunter. He told her, "I thought you were a boy."

She nodded, not at all upset. "Most folks do, at first. Pa will be here pretty soon. He and me got tied up in some business at the feed store and he sent me on ahead to meet you. Hold your horses. He won't be long. Then we'll go to our spread. Ma's lookin' forward to havin' you. We don't get much company where we are."

Abel asked, "Why do you dress like a boy?"

"It's easier for helping out with all the ranch chores we got to do. Skirts get in the way." She shrugged. "I wear 'em sometimes, though, when Ma makes me. She says I got to wear skirts to go to school in town." She turned to me. "Bethany, Ma's glad of your comin' for another reason other than company. Pa and her say you've got a whole five months to help me do something."

"What's that?"

"Teach me to read better'n a fourth-grader so I can be in the sixth grade with you when school starts."

Fourth grade! She was my age and only a fourth-grader?

She went on. "Ma sent away for McGuffey schoolbooks and tried to teach me at home, but I never got farther than book four. She gave up on me in reading, though I did good enough in arithmetic. I take to figures. We're countin' on you to have me ready in my readin', too. We don't want me to be like Pa, who has trouble with big words he reads."

Before I could tell her that I'd never taught anybody reading, Pa said, "Why, of course, Mattywill. Bethany will be happy to help you with your reading."

Now that was not one bit true! I'd expected to ride horses

27

here, not sit cooped up in a parlor with McGuffey readers I knew by heart all summer long. Frog warts! The things preacher's kids had to do that other kids didn't! Last spring I'd got a raspy sore throat from reading for hours to a whiny girl I'd never liked at school who was in bed with a busted leg. Pa had told her mother that I'd be happy to sit with her. And Abel nearly drowned last summer when Pa had promised a boy that my brother would teach him to swim. When that boy grabbed Abel around the neck and pulled him under, I'd jumped in the creek and saved both of them, even though I couldn't swim.

Though anger flared up in me, I found myself saying, "All right, but it's something I never did before, so don't expect me to be good at it." And I'd looked forward to meeting Mattywill. What was I getting myself into?

❧ 3 ❧

THE
THIRD THING

Uncle Luke was small and dark like Mama, but he didn't resemble her much except around the eyes. Yet he was a well-favored man. He shook hands with Pa, then hugged him. After that he hugged Abel and me. His voice was higher than Pa's as he told us, "Well, I'm sure glad to see you all. Reva's waitin' at home with everything ready. Come on now, let's get up into the wagon and head for home."

I bent down for my heavy valises, but Mattywill had hold of them, saying, "They're light as a feather. What you got in 'em, air? Come on. We'll sit in back on the sacks. I'll tie

29

my horse to the wagon so he can come along behind us."

And that's how we left Prineville: going over a bridge that spanned a shallow, yellow river. Later we passed a lake that was as blue as could be, reflecting the sky.

"What's the lake called, Mattywill?" I asked.

"Boone Lake, after the first white man that ever settled here. He wasn't Daniel Boone. This Boone got scalped by Comanche Indians a long time back. The lake was on an old Indian war trail. Boone had a cabin there, but the Indians burned it down. Grandpa and Grandma Thomas, Ma's folks, were the second folks to come here after old man Boone."

Abel asked in awe, "Did you fight off Indians, too?"

"Nope, Grandpa Thomas made friends with them instead. He gave 'em a steer now and then. Winters were hard on Indians. There was a U.S. Army fort here soon after Mr. Boone got scalped but the army moved out before I was born. They wasn't needed anymore." Mattywill had found a piece of straw from the wagon bottom and was chewing on it.

Abel got one and was chewing, too, as he asked, "Don't you ever see Indians anymore at all?"

"Sometimes in Prineville but the town's building too fast to suit 'em." Abel finally stopped asking questions, and Mattywill turned to me. "Bethany, to tell you truly, I ain't lookin' forward to goin' to school. I can see you're pretty book-learned by the way you look and talk."

I said, "Mama set store on book learning." I hadn't liked the tone of my cousin's voice.

She asked, "What good'll it do ya?"

"I like it. It gives me something to think about besides myself. It makes me happy sometimes."

She shrugged. "I can't say as I understand that. Give me a horse. That's all I want—me and my horse, Boots, there."

As we bounced along I told her, "I've been looking forward to riding a horse to school with you. Pa said there'd be horses for Abel and me."

"Yep, there will be. We got two critters for you two. They won't buck you off even if you can't ride at all. One's got a pleasant nature and the other don't care two hoots about anything but oats."

Abel asked, "What's mine called?"

"Little Brown Jug. Bethany's is the Deacon." She chuckled. "He's named after a man that lives in Prineville named Deacon Cass."

"Who's he, Mattywill?"

"The galoot that's supposed to be collectin' money for the church your pa will preach in. They're gonna order it by U.S. mail on the railroad as soon as the Deacon gets enough money."

"By mail?"

"That's the best way—bring the lumber in on the railroad. It'll come sawed up with plans telling how to nail it together like the picture in the catalog. Deacon Cass is lookin' to collect enough money for a church with a steeple and a bell inside it, too."

Mattywill squinted at the sun when I asked, "How much has he got now?"

She said, "I dunno. Pa says not enough by a long shot, though. The Deacon goes into saloons to pass the hat for money, and lots of times he don't come out right away."

Frog warts! I knew what that meant. Demon rum and devil whiskey. "Does our pa know about this?"

Mattywill twisted around to look at Pa and Uncle Luke on the wagon seat. So did I. Pa's shoulders appeared to be sagging. I'd heard the men talking low all along. Now I figured I knew what Uncle Luke had been telling Pa.

Mattywill's dark eyes met mine as we turned back. Waggling the straw in her mouth, she said, "That was the first thing Pa had in mind to tell your pa—how the collecting was going."

Abel asked, "How come you let a galoot like him collect for our church?"

This made our cousin laugh. She told us, "He's the son of the mayor of Prineville. They say the mayor always hankered after a preacher in his family. He had a passel of girls but just one boy. He named him Deacon, hopin' he'd get the idea to be a parson when he grew up." She scooted closer to me. "Say, when did Uncle Nat decide to be a minister?"

"Pa had a call to be one when he was seventeen."

"Who called him?"

"Mama said it was somebody inside his head."

Mattywill froze. "Is that how it is with parsons?"

"Mama said that's how it is. They get called."

What a look Mattywill gave me! "They hear words in their skulls that ain't said out loud into their ears?" She shook her head and changed the subject to ranches and cows and horses, but I knew what had gone through her skull all right. She was thinking Pa was maybe loco. My pa wasn't one bit crazy. How could she think such a thing about him? I was vexed with her for it. She wasn't turning out to be what I had expected.

Neither was the Morris ranch. It was huge! Uncle Luke had driven the wagon a long way past a lonesome wood post when Mattywill suddenly told us, "We're on our land now, ever since we passed that old piece of stumpwood. It ain't far to the house—just over the rise ahead."

Abel asked, "Where are the horses and cows? I don't see anything but grass."

This made our cousin laugh. "Cows don't run around in herds. Just a few of 'em stay together. Horses do run in herds, though. There's some wild ones south of here, but we keep the broken ones in corrals. You sure don't have much cow sense, Abel."

"I grew up in a town, Mattywill."

I was tempted to say that she didn't appear to me to have any town sense, but I bit back the words. It was up to us to get along with the Morrises since they were taking us in for God knew how long till there was a new church and a manse. And once Pa had started on his circuit riding, Abel and I would be alone with them.

Uncle Luke's house wasn't much like the two-story white one we'd had in Blue Fork. This was a long, low adobe brick building with unpainted wooden posts all along the edges of the front porch. Except for the black sheet-iron roof, it was all the same pale brown color. Behind it were other buildings of different sizes. Between them I spied a corral made out of wood railings, and milling around inside it were horses—bays and sorrels and chestnuts, blacks and grays. Hurray!

A tall dark-haired lady in a blue dress and a long white apron came running through a flock of white chickens to meet us. She cried out, "Nathaniel, welcome! Bethany, Abel, I'm your Aunt Reva."

Pa was the first one down, and she hugged him and cried on his shoulder. Then she hugged me and Abel. She smelled of cinnamon and had a nice face, a little bit freckly, with green eyes. She told us all, "I'm so glad you came. We've been looking forward to having you." Suddenly she noticed the black clothes Abel and I had worn since Mama's funeral and said, "Nathaniel, it's been four months since Dulcie's death. When can the children stop wearing mourning?"

"When six months have gone by, Reva. Then they can wear regular clothes, but with black arm bands. All they fetched here was black."

"All right. By the time they start to school, I'll have

sewed new things for them," said Aunt Reva.

Well, that made me take to Aunt Reva right off. Much as I loved and missed Mama, I hated wearing only black and feeling like an old crow. People stared at Abel and me, and ladies clucked at us like hens to show that they were sorry for us.

While Uncle Luke and Mattywill took the wagon to the barn, Aunt Reva led us into the house. It was barer inside there than in our old house. There was some heavy, home-made-looking furniture, rag rugs, and, beside the big stone fireplace, a carved wooden cradle. Billy Bob was in it. He was chubby with black hair and dark eyes, not fair like our baby had been.

While I felt the stabbings of jealousy in my head, Pa said quietly, "He looks to be a fine healthy piece of goods, Reva."

"He's a good baby, Nathaniel." Aunt Reva put her arm around Abel and said, "This is a fine healthy piece of goods, too."

"Yes, Abel's a good boy."

Aunt Reva smiled. "What about Bethany, here?"

"Bethany behaves herself." And Pa smiled at me. "You'll find that Bethany'll be a big help to you. I don't think there's a lazy bone in her body, and I doubt if she's ever told a lie in her life."

This made me blush, thinking back on Queen Fareeta. I hadn't actually lied about her, but then, I hadn't told the truth, either. I said, "Aunt Reva, I promised to help get

35

Mattywill ready for the sixth grade come fall."

My aunt smiled at me. "I expect that you and she will be the best of friends by that time. Mattywill has run wild at times. She can learn a lot from you, Bethany, girl things like embroidery and tatting."

Abel asked, "Can't she cook?"

"Not too well. She doesn't take too well to household chores. She knows as much about horses and cows as most boys hereabouts. Sometimes I think she's more like a boy than a girl."

In my heart I agreed with my aunt. I wasn't eager to teach Mattywill embroidery and tatting because I wasn't so handy with those things myself.

Aunt Reva now said, "Bethany, I'll take you to your room so you can take off your bonnet and shawl. You'll be sharing a room with Mattywill."

I followed her into a room that had two beds with red, black, and white Indian blankets on them. There was a little mirror on the wall and, below it, a washstand with a plain white pitcher and bowl. There wasn't any wardrobe, just a row of nails on the wall to hang things on. This wasn't like my nice old room, which had had blue-and-white pillows and a blue-and-red-patchwork quilt, and blue-and-white curtains, and bright-colored pictures of the Holy Land on the walls.

My surprise must have shown, because Aunt Reva explained, "Mattywill likes it like this. She won't have pretty quilts on the beds. Would you like one? You can have a rose-and-yellow one that I made."

"Please, Aunt, I would."

"Good, remind me about it after supper." And out she hurried.

I went over to the mirror and took off my bonnet. For a spell I looked at my tangled, uncombed hair and my face dirty from traveling so far. Then I stuck my tongue out at myself, put my hands on my hips, and stomped quietly. Tonight I'd start praying as hard as ever I could that the mayor's son, Deacon Cass, would be lucky and collect money as fast as greased lightning, to get Pa a church in Prineville and a house next door to it with a room for me.

There were ten of us at the big table for the welcoming chicken supper. There were the three Brants, the three Morrises, and the four Morris cowboys who had come in that night from the bunkhouse to meet us. All of them were sort of long-haired and whiskery and not too clean-looking in greasy leather vests. Two of them had been Rough Riders in Teddy Roosevelt's cavalry in Cuba during the just-ended Spanish American War. They looked to me like they could all do with a nice long soak in the lake we'd passed by that afternoon. And their table manners! I couldn't take my eyes away from the grabbing and snatching and knife spearing that went on. Mattywill didn't eat much better than the cowboys did. I hoped I wouldn't have to teach her manners, too.

I found out right away what my life was going to be like on the Morris ranch. Because I was there now, Mattywill was let off all her house chores to do boy's work. Uncle Luke said it was because she was almost as good as any man with animals.

During the daytime, while Pa, Uncle Luke, Mattywill, and Abel were outside with the hired cowboys doing men's work, I was inside doing women's work with my aunt. And there was plenty to do, too. Men's work was to tend to the horses, ride out to inspect newborn calves on the range, and mend fences. Women's work on Mondays was baking bread and afterward boiling the laundry in copper boilers on the cook stove and hanging everything outside on a clothesline. Tuesday was ironing day with seven-pound irons heated on the stove. Other days I helped black the two stoves Aunt Reva took so much pride in. Though we had a pump in our Blue Fork kitchen, Aunt Reva still used the well. She and I fetched buckets of water from it all day long, and they weighed thirty pounds full. Even with a pulley, getting a bucket of water up was hard work. Aunt Reva told me that years of heavy water pulling had made many a Texas woman round-shouldered even while she was still young. I hoped that wasn't going to happen to me.

She and I worked side by side all day long except for Sunday. During the day the only time we really rested was when she was nursing the baby. Then she sat in a rocking chair while I put my feet up on a stool.

Truthfully, though I worked hard with Aunt Reva, the bad part of each day came after supper when it was time for me to give Mattywill her lessons. Every night after we ate, we put in two hours by lamplight at the kitchen table. Mattywill was quick with numbers. She took to arithmetic just fine because she said she thought of numbers as being herds of steers for sale. She could figure as good as any fifth-grader ought to, but she was poor in spelling and could only read up through the first three McGuffey readers without falling all over the longer words. I used the fourth and fifth readers to drill her. Over and over I made her read whole paragraphs out loud of good stories with morals to them. They were the stories I'd liked in Blue Fork.

I found out that Mattywill couldn't truly read words that had more than seven letters in them, even when I split them up into two or three parts and had her go over them again and again. And how she fought me over them! One night, for instance, the word *proboscis* made her mad as hops. It was in the piece I had her read out loud from the fourth reader. It was a story about elephants, so I was naturally interested in it.

Mattywill asked me glumly, "Why don't the book say elephant's *nose* when it means *nose?* Why does it have to be a diff'runt word in this here book?"

I was patient. "Because it's a book for older kids to read. The older a kid gets, the harder the books get and the bigger the words. That's how it ought to be." Then I told her something Mama had said Mr. McGuffey had truly said.

"There's no excellence without great labor."

She didn't like hearing that. She fumed, "Oh, I don't see it that way. I don't need to read about noses and snouts on critters or about old Robinson Crusoe living in a habitation instead of a house. The start of that story says the word *house*, so why does it say *habitation* in the next line when all it means is *house*?"

That was how it went with the fourth reader. Once we got into the fifth one, every night saw us wrangling even worse over words. She was stubborn, and I got stubborn, too, and we were both weary and ready for bed when the two hours were over.

Something else got my nanny, too. I was kept so busy with the inside chores and teaching her that I didn't get onto the Deacon's back more than twice that summer, and then just in the corral. I was jealous both of Abel and Mattywill for being out riding while I was doing housework.

The tail end of May, Pa saddled up the good bay horse Uncle Luke lent him, put saddlebags filled with clothes, bedding, and his Bible onto him, and told us that it was time for him to start on his circuit now that the spring weather seemed to be holding up.

Abel and I knew what that meant. He'd be gone for months and not come back to us until early fall. Uncle Luke and Aunt Reva would have the care of us now.

Just before he rode out, Pa talked with the two of us out

on the veranda. He said, "I'm sorry I couldn't stay on in Blue Fork where we had a manse, but I couldn't do my work there anymore. You two behave yourselves. Remember who you are and what you are. Don't give your mama's kinfolks any trouble. By wintertime, the Lord willing, we may have a house of our own in Prineville."

I had to know, so I asked, "Is Deacon Cass getting the money together for your church?"

Pa nodded. "He promised that he'd keep on trying hard. He says he's got an idea or two on how to collect it faster. Well, it's in his hands—and his father's. The mayor looks to be a fine man."

I took note that Pa hadn't said the same about Deacon Cass, but I kept that to myself.

Abel and I kissed Pa, then he mounted up and headed away on the prairie trail that headed north. We watched him until he came to a rise. At the top of it he turned around, waved once to us, then went down over it and out of sight.

I put my arm around Abel's shoulder, and we Brants stood silently for a while, together. Finally, to cheer him up and myself, too, I told him, "Pa will be sure to write us wherever there's a post office. He'll be traveling in a big wide loop all over. There's bound to be lots of places with post offices. All we have to do is wait for the first letter."

Abel was quiet for a spell before he said, "When I told one of the cowboys about Pa and us leavin' Blue Fork, he

41

said Pa must be a quitter to give up a good place in a town for circuit riding. Mattywill heard what he said and didn't say one word in praise of Pa."

I sighed. Because I was older, I reckoned I understood Pa's reasons better than Abel did. I had to help Abel because now I was the only family he had here. "Abel, Pa felt the call to move on. Did you tell 'em that?"

"I didn't think of that word, but Mattywill should have."

"It ain't in her way of thinking." No, that wasn't a thing she would understand. My cousin was as different from me as night was from daytime. We weren't foes, but we weren't friends, either. In the room we shared, we didn't have much to say to each other.

Abel went on. He told me, "Mattywill tells folks you think she's dumb because she ain't so good at schoolwork as you are. That sticks in her craw."

What could I say to that? Nothing! After all, I guess I did think she was sort of dumb. Besides, it hadn't been my idea to teach her.

That night Abel and I sat sad and quiet at supper missing Pa. Aunt Reva served up chicken again to cheer us, but it didn't do much good. Her talking about being a girl pioneer afraid of wolves in winter didn't, either. It just seemed to me that she'd had a lot more fun than I had ever had.

Just as we were all about to go to bed after the supper and the McGuffey reader work, Uncle Luke's youngest cowboy came riding up to the veranda, yelling, "Hey, Mr. Morris. Mr. Morris!"

"That'd be Tad," said Uncle Luke. "I sent him to town for my mail. He sounds like he's hit a couple of saloons on the way home."

Tad didn't get off his horse and come inside. He stayed out in front of the house, and kept shouting, so we all came out onto the veranda. Aunt Reva was peeved with him because his yelling had woken Billy Bob up. She called out to Tad, "What's the matter with you, boy? Are you drunk?"

"Not too much, missus." Tad leaned from his saddle with a handful of paper for Uncle Luke. He said, "Here's some letters for you. I come to tell you there's somethin' interestin' comin' to Prineville on the railroad the Fourth of July you ought to know about. I just heard about it."

I held my breath, hoping. Could this be the lumber for the new church and our manse? But no, Pa would have told us if that was about to happen. Besides, Tad wouldn't be interested in church doings.

Uncle Luke asked, "What's that you heard, Tad?"

"By Jiminy, a real circus, that's what. It'll be one fine and dandy Fourth of July this year. I seen a colored picture. It had pretty ladies and lions and striped tigers and everything—even them great big critters, the ones with big ears and long teeth out front and noses so long they fall on the ground. I seen 'em all in the picture put on the saloon wall."

Elephants? He meant *elephants.* I clapped one hand over my mouth to keep from yelling while I clutched at the nearest porch post with the other. Elephants in Prineville! Queen Fareeta had struck again!

❧ 4 ❧

DEACON CASS
AND HIS
MONEYMAKING PLANS

By mid-June the roundup, branding, and gelding were done, as well as spring housecleaning. With these chores out of the way, Aunt Reva finally decided that the ranch could spare us for one Saturday afternoon and we could come into town with her when she went to buy some things at the General Store she didn't trust Uncle Luke or a cowboy to get for her.

All of us, including Billy Bob, went to Prineville. Uncle Luke, Aunt Reva, and the baby rode in the wagon. Mattywill and Abel rode horseback, and Uncle Luke thought I ought to, too, to get in practice sitting a horse before school started. I didn't have trousers, so Aunt Reva made Mattywill loan me a pair of hers. They were a mite tight and too long, but after rolling them up I did all right getting onto the Deacon. He was a dun-colored horse with a yellow flop of hair over his forehead, yellow eyes, a scraggly yellow mane, and a long, skinny face.

He didn't seem inclined to travel, so all the way into town he moseyed behind the wagon and the other two horses. He ate dust and I ate dust. His head sagged lower and lower no matter how often I dug into him with my heels to keep up with the others. If he was going to be this way next fall, I'd have to start out for school a whole hour earlier than my brother and cousin. And I'd thought riding a horse would be a whole lot of fun. The Deacon sure wasn't!

The town had been built up plenty since we'd gotten off the train here weeks before. Where we'd seen boards standing up on their ends then, we saw houses and stores now. Most of the new ones weren't painted yet, but I reckoned that'd be next.

Mayor Cass, a portly man with an elk's tooth on his gold watch chain, came down off a boardwalk with his hand out to greet Uncle Luke and Aunt Reva. I heard him say, "That's a fine, bouncing lad you've got there, Missus Morris. He's prime goods."

Aunt Reva laughed and said, "Thank you. How's your family, Mayor?"

"The girls is fine. I'm marryin' 'em off one by one to farmers hereabouts."

Now Uncle Luke asked, "How is Deacon Cass doing?"

He motioned toward Abel and me. "By the way, the yellow-headed kids are Preacher Brant's two."

"Well, well, pleased to meet ya." Mayor Cass came over to us and shook our hands. His was pink and damp.

I noted that the mayor hadn't answered Uncle Luke's question. Instead he said to me, "You'll be goin' to school here come September, I reckon. We're lookin' high and low for a teacher. The lumber's come in on the railroad for the schoolhouse, and it'll start goin' up soon."

I asked, "What about the wood for our pa's church?"

The mayor looked at his pocket watch. "It ain't been sent for as yet."

Now Aunt Reva asked, "You mean that money hasn't been collected yet?"

"No, ma'am, but it's comin' in all the time. My boy's gatherin' it right along. He's at it right now. He ought to be out among us any minute now. I went in and told him to come out the minute I saw you folks headin' this way." Mayor Cass turned his head to the left and pointed, then said, "There's Deacon, now."

I didn't need to be told which man coming through the swinging doors of the Red Slipper Saloon was Deacon Cass. Even dressed up in a yellow-and-black-checkered suit, wearing a black derby hat and shining black shoes, he did indeed resemble the horse I was riding. He had a yellow mustache, a long skinny face, and a flop of yellow hair sticking out from under his hat. And when his pa hollered to him to come over to us, I saw that his eyes were so pale a brown that they were almost yellow, too.

Deacon Cass stopped, smelling to high heaven of bay rum shaving lotion, right next to me and my horse. I heard Mattywill giggling and felt sorry for both Deacon Cass and the horse.

"How're you doin' on the fund for the church and the preacher's house?" his pa asked him.

"I can't complain. They gave me five dollars in silver in there." Seeing Aunt Reva look disapprovingly at him, he took off his hat and addressed her. "I know you think it's strange, ma'am, that I collect for a noble cause in saloons, but that's where the most loose money is in a boomtown, you know."

"I would *not* know that," said Aunt Reva, sitting up straighter than usual.

Mayor Cass went over to her side of the wagon to say, "Now, ma'am, we got to get the money any way we can. Most folks here have put all the money they've got into farm equipment and animals or into building up a business. They haven't got much spare cash. Tell you what, my wife's at the General Store. Why don't you and the kids go over there and show her that fine baby of yours. She'd be tickled to death to admire him while Luke and my boy and I wash the dust out of our throats."

Uncle Luke said, "That's a good idea, Mister Mayor. Reva, I'll take the wagon and leave it at the emporium, then walk back down here."

Though my aunt sniffed, she didn't argue about Uncle

47

Luke going into a saloon. Just as we passed the mayor and Deacon Cass, the mayor cried out after us, "That was a jim-dandy, hell-roarin' sermon your pa delivered in the Red Slipper just before he left on his circuit."

I gasped. Pa had preached here in a saloon? That seemed almost as bad as my going inside Queen Fareeta's tent.

I'd been thinking of her all morning and kept my eyes peeled the minute we got to the edge of town for the circus posters the cowboy Tad had talked about.

Finally I spotted one on the side wall of the saloon next to the General Store. My, but it was the most color-filled piece of paper I'd ever set eyes on. As soon as I tied Deacon to the hitching rack, I ran over to admire it. It was a crowded poster, full of acrobats, lions and tigers, acrobatic bears— and elephants. The poster showed seven elephants standing up on their hind legs leaning on each other's backs with their trunks up in the air. A grinning blond lady in rose-colored tights stood in front of them with her arms held high, showing how big they were and how small she was.

Abel and Mattywill joined me to stare at the poster. "Jiminy," breathed Abel, "it's really coming here."

"Yep, on the Fourth of July," said Mattywill excitedly. "And Pa and Ma said I could come. I wouldn't have to stay home with Billy Bob. Abel'll be comin' too. Mama wouldn't leave him alone with the baby."

In all that I hadn't once heard my name. My heart started its fall down toward my shoes. Mattywill hadn't said so straight out, but it appeared to me that she was saying I'd be the one who had to stay behind and mind Billy Bob.

After my heart finished falling, my temper started to rise. Like yeast in bread dough, it swelled up in my chest, nearly choking me. My cousin was getting all the good, and I was getting all the bad, and that wasn't fair. Could I carry my cross like a good preacher's girl ought to? Could I stay home and not feel mean about staying when Abel and Mattywill got to go? Frog warts. Elephants could be important to me. Queen Fareeta had told me so. Somehow I had to get to Prineville on the Fourth of July.

Leaving Abel and Mattywill staring at the poster, I turned around and marched into the General Store. Like all general stores, it was crowded with all sorts of things, from yards of calico, to butter churns, to plows and harness pieces. Aunt Reva was standing near the pickle barrels among a crowd of ladies who were making clucking noises at Billy Bob and admiring him.

A distance away from Aunt Reva stood a redheaded, freckly lady with a baby in her arms, too, glaring daggers at Aunt Reva.

Wondering why, I went up to her and asked, "May I see your baby? Is it a her or a him?"

"Benjamin's a boy. Have a look at the handsomest baby boy in town. I ought to know. I'm his mama." Now she grinned as she opened the blanket. I peeked. Benjamin was red-faced and red-haired, like his mother. Just then he opened a big red mouth in a howl that made Billy Bob howl, too. No, I couldn't say Benjamin was handsome as the lady thought he was.

She shouted to me over all the baby noises. "I'm Mrs. Mack. My husband's the new barber here. My Benjamin's going to be *the* baby in the pageant here at Christmas. I just know it. The mayor's son is going to be selling tickets at a nickel apiece during the Fourth of July celebration so folks can vote for the baby in the manger. The money goes toward the new church we're going to have."

I drew back fast. First collecting money in saloons and now selling tickets to vote for the Baby Jesus? That Deacon Cass. He had some real strange ideas.

I asked, "Are there other babies in the running?"

"Uh-huh, there are three others, all boys, of course. No girls can enter." Mrs. Mack was still glaring at Aunt Reva. "One of those women over there just told that lady with the black-haired baby that she ought to enter him. That'd make five boys in the race."

She meant Billy Bob! Not telling her who I was, I asked, "What did the lady say?"

"She laughed and said she would think about it. There'll be hundreds of folks comin' here the Fourth of July, and Deacon Cass has got town kids all lined up, ready to help him. Two of my older children will be selling tickets, too. I just hope Deacon don't drink up or gamble away the church money. He's a sure enough poker hound."

Gambling? Poker? Cards? Sinful stuff, all of 'em! This was an awful way to go about getting money for the church. I wished with all my heart that Pa was here right now to do something about Deacon Cass.

Hearing enough for now, I ran out to where Abel and Mattywill were sitting on the top step eating licorice-stick candy. Uncle Luke had given her a penny for three sticks. After she handed me mine, I told her and Abel what Mrs. Mack had said about the Christmas pageant. Abel looked surprised at this, but Mattywill took it in her stride.

"Now that would be real fine," she said, "wouldn't it? That's a dandy idea. I'd like for Billy Bob to be the baby in the manger. All he has to do is lay there and look handsome."

Abel asked, "Will they be needing any angels? Bethany was an angel in a pageant. She did just fine. She flew on ropes. Pa said she looked just beautiful."

Angel? I let out a sigh. Yes, I'd been one in Blue Fork, where I was hoisted up on ropes across the back of our church. I couldn't honestly say I'd enjoyed it, though.

Mattywill gave me a hard look, and what she said came out almost like a snarl. "A angel, huh? That figures. You got yellow hair, and you're a preacher's kid, so you get to be a angel. Black-headed girls don't get to be angels, I suppose."

I was feeling sort of tickled that my being an angel had riled her so, but before I could answer her, she changed the subject. "You say we have to sell tickets so Billy Bob can be little Jesus?"

"That's right, Mattywill. The most ticketed baby wins."

Abel told her, "The three of us could sell tickets, but livin' way out where we do, only the cowboys'll buy them, I guess."

This didn't faze our cousin. "No, not out there. We'll sell 'em at the Fourth of July celebration here in town, like the other kids will be doin'. All three of us'd have to work hard, but we could sell plenty, I bet. Pa knows a lot of farmers and ranchers who'll be comin' in then. They'll put out some nickels on Billy Bob for sure."

Aha! Mattywill had just said "the three of us." Now was the moment for me to speak up if I wanted to come in for the Fourth of July celebration.

I said, "Your mama had better come here with Billy Bob for sure on the Fourth, so folks can get a real good gander at him. Folks would wonder if she left him behind."

Mattywill nodded. "You're right there. I'll tell Pa about the Baby Jesus vote. He'd like seeing Billy Bob have the big part in the pageant. It'll be the first one we ever had in Prineville. They've been talkin' about it since last winter. They're going to clear out the General Store and put up a sort of platform. The store's plenty high enough for an angel to come down from the rafters on ropes. Say, Bethany, did you get lowered down or did you slide?"

Abel explained. "She sort of slid."

I said, "No, I got dropped."

Mattywill ignored that remark. "Abel, what were you in the pageant at your church?"

"I started out two years ago as a sheep, but last year I was the smallest shepherd, me and some girls."

"Well," Mattywill replied with a laugh, "maybe you'll graduate to a donkey this year."

Abel didn't think that was funny any more than I did, so neither one of us laughed.

In a couple of hours Uncle Luke and Aunt Reva had bought what they needed in the way of supplies: kerosene, sugar, thread, new sewing machine needles, flour, and some horse medicines. Then we left for the ranch.

I was smarter on the trip home. I tethered Deacon to the wagon, so he had to keep up with it. Abel and Mattywill rode in front of it.

As I bounced along beside the wagon I thought about the Fourth of July. I thought hard, remembering how Pa sometimes said the Lord helps those who help themselves.

I called out to Aunt Reva, who was on my side of the wagon. "I met a lady in the General Store who told me she's entering her baby boy in the Baby Jesus contest at the Fourth of July celebration."

"Oh, yes, Bethany, that'd be Mrs. Mack, the barber's wife."

Stretching the truth a little, I said, "She's got a mighty handsome baby with lots of red hair."

"Handsome, is he?" asked my aunt. She sounded a mite

annoyed. "Well, I really didn't look at him." She added, "I
sure heard him, though."

Knowing I was being sly and feeling sort of guilty about
it, I told her, "Oh, he's good-lookin', all right."

Now I saw her open Billy Bob's blanket to look at his
sleeping face. She asked me, "Would you say he's hand-
somer than Billy Bob, Bethany?"

I told her slowly, "Well, of course, *I* don't think so. After
all, Billy Bob's my blood cousin. Mrs. Mack did say that
some ladies were asking you to enter Billy Bob in the contest. Are you?"

"Oh, I don't know, Bethany, even if it is for a good
cause."

"Why not, Reva?" came from Uncle Luke, who was
slapping the reins on the team's rumps. "It'll be our duty to
do it to get money for Nate's church. The more babies in
the race, the better, I say."

Was I glad to hear him say that! I sort of figured he
might because he was so proud of Billy Bob. I went on fast,
"Deacon Cass is going to be sellin' tickets at a nickel apiece.
The baby with the most tickets sold gets the manger. I already told Mattywill and Abel about it. The three of us are
going to sell tickets on the Fourth of July so Billy Bob'll
win. We can, can't we?"

Uncle Luke called out to me, "I don't see why not,
Bethany."

"But Aunt Reva'll have to fetch Billy Bob to town that
day. Folks who buy tickets ought to get to see him before

they shell out for him. We'll *all* of us have to go."

He told me laughing, "Then all of us *will* go. Nobody'll run away with the ranch in one day."

Glory be, I was going! I'd done it! I looked at the bright blue sky overhead and, like the Bible says, I "rejoiced." It was true that the Lord helps those who help themselves— even if it takes some doing.

⛤ 5 ⛤

LADY PEACHES

It seemed to me that the six weeks to the Fourth of July went by, moving as slow as my horse. Aunt Reva and I did the same old chores in the house while the menfolk and Mattywill worked in the barn, corral, and on the open range miles from the house. At night I drilled Mattywill in parsing sentences.

About the only things that happened were that Billy Bob grew some and got pinker-cheeked, and Abel and I got a letter from Pa.

The letter didn't say too much—only that he was well and had performed three weddings and four baptizings in his travels. He'd had some successes, too, with backsliders

who hadn't been to a church in years and years. He wrote
us from where he'd been in the middle of June, a place way
north of Prineville, and he asked us to write him where he
planned to be the middle of August. I tried to find the place
he named on a map of Texas, but it wasn't there.

I answered his letter right off. I told him we all felt fine
and wrote about the Glorious Fourth and the circus coming.
I told him that Deacon Cass was still collecting for our
church and manse but didn't say any more about it. I didn't
mention the big Christmas baby race, either, because I
wasn't at all sure how Pa would take to the idea. I signed
my letter with love and put lots of *X*'s on it, then I got Abel
to add some more of them and write a few lines about how
he loved his horse, Little Brown Jug. I couldn't bring myself to write kindly of my critter, so I left him out altogether.

Oh, but I was excited the night of July third. I could
hardly sleep, I was so full of thinking about the next day.
Because it would be summer-hot, I planned, to wear the
pale-blue-and-white-checkered gingham dress Aunt Reva
had just made on her sewing machine. She had also made
me a sunbonnet out of what was left over of the cloth. It
was a jim-dandy outfit and I loved it. This would be the first
time I wouldn't be wearing black, but all the same, Abel and
I wore a black crepe band on our right arms to show respect
for Mama.

Mattywill had a red-and-white-checkered gingham outfit.
She didn't take to it because it had a skirt, not trousers, and

she hated the long stockings and girl's high-top button shoes she had to wear.

Aunt Reva had sewed a white-and-blue-striped shirt for Abel and another for Uncle Luke. For herself she had made a white muslin dress with an ivory-colored lace bertha collar. We all looked just fine as we headed for town in the wagon, with the cowboys riding on ahead, and behind us, on horseback.

I was so excited, I could scarcely sit still in the back of the wagon. Mattywill gave me a glare when I accidentally booted her once as she sat with one arm over our big picnic basket.

She growled, "Save some of that pep you got, Bethany, to sell tickets. You'll need it. First thing of all, we have to get hold of Deacon Cass and get us a bunch of tickets. He ought to be easy to find somewheres near Boone Lake."

I nodded. The Fourth of July events and the circus would be held at Boone Lake, not Prineville, because of the fireworks. Scared of setting fire to the new town, Mayor Cass had decided it would be safer if they were set off from a raft out in the lake.

We weren't the first folks at the lake by a long shot. There were wagons, buckboards, and surreys all over. Folks had spread blankets and quilts on the grass. Barbecuing was going on in pits in the ground—and probably had been all night long. Neither this nor the rodeo interested me, though. What I wanted to see was the circus. I spotted the big red-and-white-striped tent right off and, next to it, large, green-painted cages on wheels—cages for the animals. But where were the elephants?

Of course, I wanted to make tracks for the circus first. I could smell it sharp in my nose the minute I got down out of the wagon. I was already headed for it before Mattywill's and Abel's feet hit the ground when Uncle Luke caught me by the shoulder and said, "Bethany, I have something for you." He took coins from his pocket and gave me three nickels. "Here's fifteen cents. A dime'll get you into the circus if you want to go."

I thanked him and asked, "Where do you think the elephants are?"

He laughed, looked at the tents, then said, "More than likely inside the tents. The size they are, it'd be hard to hide 'em. I don't see any."

Thanking him once more, I started again for the big tents. This time Mattywill grabbed me by one of my long curls and hauled me back to her. She told me in a hiss, "You stay here. We find Deacon Cass first, remember? We're going to look for him together while Ma finds us a good place to put our blankets down to sit on."

Even though my head ached where she'd yanked my curl, I had to admit that she was right. So the three of us started scouting the banks of the lake for Deacon Cass.

He wasn't hard to find. His pa, the mayor, all duded up for the day in a white linen suit, was standing on top of a grandstand built close to the water's edge. Deacon, all in white, too, was talking to some younger men beneath it as they leaned against the red, white, and blue bunting.

Mattywill trotted right up to them and spoke her piece to Deacon Cass. "Me and my cousins intend to sell tickets so my baby brother gets to be the Baby Jesus. We need some tickets." Then she tacked on "please."

Deacon didn't seem to mind her being so pushy. He grinned. "Sure, Matt. How many do you want? This is the only day folks can vote for the Baby Jesus with a ticket because we'll never get so many folks all together in one place again. Pa and me have got to think about the pageant all the rest of the year and not be selling tickets for it. We—"

My cousin didn't let him finish. "Who's ahead?"

"Baby Mack. The way I figure it, he's got one hundred and two tickets to his credit. The contest ends today at sundown. You'll have to sell fast to beat him out. His sisters have been out sellin' for an hour already. They got the green tickets. There are yellow and blue and white ones for the other babies. Your baby brother will be a red ticket kid."

Mattywill frowned and said, "Well, give me two hundred and fifty red ones. We'll split 'em up to sell."

"Sure. I got 'em right here." Deacon Cass reached into his coat pocket and brought out a bright red roll. Counting fast, he gave Mattywill the number of tickets she'd asked for and told her, "Bring back what you don't sell along with the money."

"I hear you, Deacon. We'll sell 'em all."

As Mattywill counted and tore off our tickets I asked him, "How're you comin' on collecting for the church?"

"Tolerably well, little sister."

"That's good," said Abel. "How much have you got?"

Cass rolled a toothpick around in his mouth, then said, "I ain't counted how much lately—but it's comin' along nicely."

By now Mattywill was shoving red tickets into Abel's and my hands with the words, "Split up. Let's hitch up our britches and get a move on. I'll go down the middle; you go right, Bethany; and you left, Abel. If they want to see Billy Bob before they cough up for a ticket on him, you send 'em to Ma to have a look. I figure we can peddle till after we eat and the circus show and rodeo begin. Most folks'll go to one or the other. We can sell during the band concert till the speeches start just before sundown. After that'll come the fireworks, when it'll be too dark to sell."

"Sure, Mattywill." I wasn't one bit unhappy that the side she'd given me was the one the circus tents were on. That's where I'd go right away.

We started off but got called back by the mayor. "Hey, you girls!" Would I never get to the circus tents?

Mattywill and I ran back to the grandstand.

The mayor leaned over the railing and handed us a tablet and pencil, saying, "Write down your names, you two. We want a little gal crowned here tonight as Miss Columbia, the Gem of the Ocean. We're goin' to draw her name out

61

of my hat later on. She'll get crowned and sit up here on the platform with two judges and a senator from the Texas legislature."

Mattywill and I looked at each other. Her eyes gleamed, and she was grinning as she wrote her name. Then I wrote mine, too, and gave the tablet and pencil back to the mayor.

Mattywill asked, "If I win, do I get to keep the crown? Is it real gold? You didn't have a Miss Columbia last year, did you?"

"This is new this year. No, the crown ain't gold, but it sparkles. If you win the draw, you got to give it back for next year. I see you're sellin' tickets for the baby derby."

"You bet—for my baby brother to win. We got to get a move on now."

After Mattywill ran off I smiled at the mayor, thanked him, and went straight to the circus tents to prowl around. There were three lions, one tiger, and two cages of big brown bears. There were lots of people moving about, too, some of them dressed up in everyday clothes and others in spangled tights.

I asked a fat little man in a black derby hat, "Where are the elephants?"

He took the cigar out of his mouth to say, "Between the tents, sis. Do you like elephants?"

"I don't know yet. They could be important to me."

"What?" He laughed. "Too bad you ain't a boy. We got five boys waterin' the elephants right now, fetching buckets from the lake. Elephants have a powerful thirst, and this day's goin' to be a scorcher. Boys who water the elephants get into the circus for free."

Though I didn't see that as one bit fair to girls, I didn't say so. I just went softly around the tent and peeked.

There they were! Five great big, gray wrinkled-looking animals with long whitish-yellow tusks and little tiny eyes. Elephants so close to me that I could walk ten steps to the nearest one, put out my hand, and touch it. I was so thrilled at the sight of them that I could hardly breathe.

The schoolbook at Blue Fork had been right. They had to be the biggest animals walking the earth, though some whales in the ocean were supposed to be bigger. Why, anytime those elephants wanted to pull up the pegs that tethered them and walk away, they could. But the book had said they were peaceful, and they looked it, swaying their trunks and rumbling to one another.

I just stood there watching them with them not even noticing me when all at once a boy came running toward one of them. He had two big buckets splashing water from their tops, and I saw him set them down in front of the biggest elephant.

He called out, "Here you be, Lady Peaches. Suck 'em up."

That elephant did, too. She dipped her long trunk into one bucket after another and sucked up the water so fast, I could hardly believe my eyes. The other elephants drank water other boys brought to them. I stood and watched those big, quiet elephants for ten minutes, forgetting all about the red tickets in my hand. All I could think about then was Queen Fareeta's words.

Finally I got hold of myself and went off to try to sell my tickets.

Mattywill, Abel, and I weren't the only kids selling in the growing crowd. There were two dark-haired boys and two redheaded girls who resembled Mrs. Mack. One of the girls gave me a dirty look when she heard me say, "I'm selling tickets for Billy Bob Morris to be the Baby Jesus at the Christmas pageant. My pa's to be the preacher in the new church the ticket you buy will help to build."

Some folks would shake their heads and show me a green or yellow or white ticket, and I'd smile and say, "I'm sorry I pestered you," but plenty of folks smiled and gave me nickels for a red one for Billy Bob.

So I went from blanket to blanket and then over to where the kids' races were going on. Lots of folks there with their kids turned out to know Aunt Reva's family as real old-timers, and they bought tickets off me. One man bought ten tickets, which I thought was very handsome of him. The pretty lady with him gave me a sweet sprig of honey-suckle to pin onto the front of my dress. Smelling sweetly of the flowers, I backed away from the lady and smack dab into Mattywill. "Get out of my middle, Bethany," she snapped, "and get back onto your own side." Then she was gone, and good riddance, too.

By the time the circus was to start, I'd sold sixty-one tickets and my pockets were jingling with money. I hoped

Mattywill and Abel were doing as well as I was.

I watched the circus show from a top row of seats. A little later on, Abel and the four Morrises came in together and sat some distance away on the other side of the ring. I didn't mind sitting alone. The show was wonderful. There were clowns and people acrobats and bear acrobats and snarling lions and tigers jumping through hoops when a handsome red-jacketed young trainer snapped his whip.

I saw a pretty red-haired lady horseback rider in purple tights gallop around the tent and do fancy tricks. She hung down out of the saddle and picked up golden balls lying on the ground. Then she stood up on the white horse's rump as he cantered along, his mane flying. She jumped off and then jumped back up onto him as he went by. I thought that lady and her horse were sure pretty, and judging by how long everyone clapped, the rest of the audience thought so, as well.

There were Indians, too, six of 'em, on spotted ponies. I think they were Sioux from up north, and they rode around all dressed up in war paint, beadwork, buckskin, and feathers. They shook their lances and cried their war cries as they rode. I'd never seen Indians like these in Blue Fork—the couple that I saw dressed like everybody else. These Indians made the riding lady's outfit kind of dull.

But it wasn't the trick rider or the Indians I'd come to see. It was the elephants. Finally they came on. While I watched them they trotted around in circles, danced on their thick hind legs, and then stood up in a row the way they were on the poster. I was even more thrilled with them than I'd been with the lion tamer, who had stuck his head in a lion's jaws full of big white teeth. I was most impressed by the biggest elephant of all, Lady Peaches. She wore a bright pink shiny cloth and gold-fringed halter on top of her head and along her back. She not only stood up on her hind legs but rose up in a bow on her front ones. How we all clapped at that! I clapped so hard, my hands hurt.

After Lady Peaches had bowed, the show was over.

I stayed where I was until all the animals and most of the people had gone out, then I came down from the top row. I was sort of disappointed. Though the elephants had been one of the grandest sights I had ever seen, Queen Fareeta had been wrong about them being any more important to me than to anybody else in the crowd.

I went outside into afternoon heat that almost knocked me down, it was so powerful. I was thirsty and my face burned. Before I tried to sell the rest of my tickets, I decided to wash up in the lake and have a drink. So I headed for the water.

That's where I was—at the lake's edge about to bend down and scoop up some water—when I heard all the terrible racket from behind me. People were yelling and screeching, but above those noises I could hear the ground rumbling. Could it be an earthquake?

I whirled around fast, and what I saw made me so scared, I came close to fainting away.

Elephants! *Running elephants!* Their feet made the

ground tremble. Ears flapping, feet pounding, snaky trunks swaying, all five circus elephants came running with Lady Peaches in the lead. Some circus men ran behind them, hollering, waving their arms. And all of them—five elephants and four men—were heading straight for me, Bethany Brant!

I couldn't move. I couldn't think. I couldn't even breathe. I was a goner for sure. I knew it. My fate was to be trampled by elephants. That was what Queen Fareeta had meant when she said they would be important to me. This was my punishment, for sure! What could be more important?

I closed my eyes and gave up my soul.

After a second I opened them again. Lady Peaches had skidded to a stop just before she ran over me. The elephant was like an animal mountain standing right next to me, looking down at me out of little deep-set eyes. Her big gray trunk came down my shoulder to nuzzle at my chest. While I froze, too scared even to pray, the trunk sniffed at my honeysuckle, tickling my chest. Then all at once it moved down to my waist, circled it, and before I knew what was happening, that trunk lifted me into the air. A second later I was plunked down on top of Lady Peaches's back, and she was crushing her way through the reeds down into Boone Lake with me aboard and with the other elephants following behind her.

Queen Fareeta had struck again!

◆§ 6 §◆

MISS COLUMBIA, THE GEM OF THE OCEAN

I was too scared to yell, too scared to do anything but hang on to the satiny pink cloth on the elephant's back while she and the others waded out belly-deep into the water. I didn't dare faint. If I did, I'd fall off for sure among big elephant bodies.

Once they were in the lake water, the elephants began to drink like they meant to suck the lake dry. They must have been thirsty as all get-out after the show in the hot, stuffy tent. Once they drank their fill, they stood still for a while, moving their ears like fans, making grumbling noises to each other. One took up a trunkful of water and sprayed another one. Seeing this made me look down at Lady

Peaches's very wide back and shiver with fear. What would happen next? The elephants weren't showing any sign of leaving the water now that they'd had themselves a drink.

I heard yelling and looked to the shoreline. It was crowded with people. I could see all of the Morrises and Abel and the mayor and Deacon Cass out front with some circus men.

One man with a megaphone yelled out to me from the grandstand, "Little girl, you out there on the elephant, you just stay where you are! Don't you say a word. Just stay there. The elephants are only thirsty."

As if I had a choice!

He hollered, "We'll get you back here safe and sound. I'm comin' out to you. Hang on to that animal."

I watched him come down off the grandstand and into the water. Lady Peaches saw him, too. She filled her trunk with water, and when he came close enough, she blasted him like the fire-engine hose I'd seen used to put out a fire in Blue Fork. Two of the other elephants also sucked up water and squirted him when he tried to get up and come forward again. They knocked him onto his back four times.

After he got up for the fifth time, he climbed back up onto the bank and yelled at the crowd. "Go back to your barbecue, folks. This elephant'll come out of the lake when she's good and ready. Don't pay the animals any heed. Don't upset 'em, please."

Don't upset the *elephants,* I thought. What about me?

The crowd did what he asked and moved off, except for

Uncle Luke, Aunt Reva, Mattywill and Abel, and the mayor, his son, and two circus men. All of them climbed up onto the grandstand, sat down on chairs, and faced me and the elephants while I sat on Lady Peaches and looked at them.

Suddenly one of the elephants rolled in the water, then two others did. I heard Aunt Reva's scream, and I felt like screaming, too. Would Lady Peaches roll and crush me under her?

She didn't. She moved out into deeper water so my feet and legs got wet, but she stood up.

Among all these elephants I felt sick to my stomach. What was going to happen to me out in this lake? Would Lady Peaches eventually take it into her head to roll or go swimming? Since I didn't weigh much, would she forget that she had me on her back? I didn't dare remind her.

I tried to put my mind on other happier things, but they wouldn't come to me. I kept seeing Pa's face, wishing he were here right now. He'd think of something to do to save me. But who knew where he was at this very minute while his only daughter was sitting scared out of her wits on the back of an elephant?

Mama came into my thoughts next, but I couldn't see her in my mind as clear as I saw him. I did seem to smell something that reminded me of her, though. Sure, the honeysuckle pinned on my dress. We'd had honeysuckle all over the veranda back in Blue Fork. Mama had loved it and sometimes stuck a piece of it in my hair and in hers, too, where it had shone yellow and white and smelled so sweet. *Oh, Mama,* my heart cried out, and I cried, too, but very softly.

And I didn't forget to pray, either. I prayed that I'd get out of this. And I told God how sorry I was for my past wickedness and for not always being grateful to be living in Mattywill's house and having the Deacon as my very own horse. I had plenty to pray about to pass the time.

The afternoon went on and on and got hotter and hotter. The elephants might have been cool, but I wasn't. I roasted and wiped tears away with my fists and kept praying. An elephant sprayed me once, and that felt almost good, though it also almost washed me off Lady Peaches's back.

Seeing that the elephants didn't seem likely to come tramping up out of Boone Lake at any minute, whole families started to come down to its banks to look at me and Lady Peaches and her friends. We were almost as good a show as the circus and rodeo had been. Besides, we didn't cost anything. I watched people spread out their quilts and blankets not far from the water's edge, and sit or loll on their elbows eating barbecue. Seeing them eating kept reminding me how hungry I was. For the most part the people kept quiet—for my sake, I hoped—but I could hear a guitar playing and some singing, too. The music came clear as could be over the water, and one elephant swayed its trunk in time to the tunes. Lady Peaches moved her big ears forward to listen, but she didn't move out toward the shore as I'd hoped.

One thing I saw from where I sat upset me. Abel and Mattywill were walking among the picnickers at the lakeside. I could see them point to me and the elephants and then turn away to talk to the people. At first I thought they were asking them to pray for me. Then I realized that they were peddling tickets! They were getting people to feel sorry for us Brants and Morrises because I was in such a pickle, and buy tickets for Billy Bob. This had to have been my cousin's idea. She'd talked Abel into doing it. I didn't think it was the right thing to do to me or the right way to get money for our church at all.

I longed to yell out over the water, "You stop that, Mattywill Morris. You stop that, Abel." But I didn't let out a peep for fear of upsetting my elephant.

At sundown that same circus man came down into the water and got himself squirted again. A few minutes later I watched him and Uncle Luke arguing with a tall man with a star on his chest who had come to the water's edge with a buffalo gun. Oh, no! He wanted to shoot Lady Peaches. Thank goodness Uncle Luke wouldn't let him try. He could have shot me instead!

Dusk came, and it was time for the band concert and speech making. But there wasn't any of that because of me. The commotion could upset the elephants. Nobody came rowing out to the raft a distance away from us with boxes of fireworks, either. I'd ruined a lot of people's Fourth of July, and Lady Peaches had sure ruined mine.

By now I ached all over from not moving a muscle for so long, and without the sun on me, I was getting cold. For the first time I dared to say something out loud. I prayed hard to the Lord to help me, then I leaned down and, hoping Lady Peaches understood English, whispered to her, "Elephant, don't you think it's time to go home?" My teeth chattered as I spoke.

She didn't move. Neither did the other elephants, and neither did I. They stood—I sat, shivering.

All of a sudden, a bright curve of red fire and a shower of scarlet, white, and green stars burst over us from the shore. I knew what it was. Someone had let off a Roman candle. I held my breath in terror as I felt Lady Peaches twitch under me.

Then she started forward. Apparently she didn't like fireworks. Slowly she came up out of Boone Lake with the other four elephants following behind her. She stopped at the edge of the water, lifted that trunk of hers, and waved it around me once more. I gasped as it felt for my midsection, then lifted me up into the air. Would she crush me?

No. She only set me on the ground. I fell into a heap and rolled away from her fast, the ticket money jingling in my deep dress pocket. From where I was on the grass I watched the elephants grab hold of each other, trunk to tail, and lumber by me back to the tent with the circus men sprinting to keep up with them.

In a minute Uncle Luke, Aunt Reva, Mattywill, Abel,

the mayor, Deacon Cass, and some other folks came running and were all around me in a circle. Now I could really cry loudly, and I did.

Uncle Luke lifted me up and held me close. "Oh, the Lord be praised. You're all right, Bethany!"

Abel hugged my back as the mayor told me, "You're a true hero, little girl. We're forgetting all about drawin' a girl's name tonight. You're goin' to be our Miss Columbia, the Gem of the Ocean." Saying this, he hurried off to tell the band to finally start playing the loud kind of music they hadn't played so as to keep the elephants quiet.

I couldn't speak over the sound of the loud brass band. Finally, though, I gasped out, "Does anybody know what that elephant wanted with me?"

Shouting over the noise, Abel answered. "The circus man said it had to be because of that honeysuckle you put on your dress. I saw that lady give it to you, and I told him about that. He said elephants can't see or hear so good, but they've got dandy smellers. He told us that a circus lady who used to ride on Lady Peaches a long time back always wore honeysuckle eau-de-cologne. You smelled like something that elephant used to know, and elephants remember things."

I was still pretty upset and kept tearing so that Mattywill yelled at me, "Stop your bawling, Bethany, you're all right."

I ignored her and said, "I need to sit down somewhere and eat something."

Aunt Reva told me, "Come along back to where we're sitting. We've got fried chicken and watermelon, and Luke'll get you some barbecue beef." My aunt helped me walk back, but not Mattywill. She went on ahead of us, lifting her feet high.

Oh, the black look on my cousin's face as she passed me. But why? She ought to be sorry for me, but she surely didn't seem to be. Suddenly Mattywill came back to us and, speaking so low that her ma couldn't hear her, hissed, "You're goin' to be the Gem of the Ocean!"

I couldn't believe my ears. She was jealous. I might have been trampled to death or drowned dead, and she was jealous! My innards began to burn with anger. I didn't care about being Miss Columbia, but she sure did.

I held my temper in as she moved off again and asked Aunt Reva, "Whose idea was the Roman candle?"

"It was the circus man's. Elephants hate fire, he says. He had to wait till near dark so the elephants would be sure to see it and run away. Come on, now. You get some food and rest, and then you'll get crowned Prineville's first Miss Columbia."

When we got to the blankets and sat down next to the lady who had been tending to Billy Bob, I told Mattywill, "I sold sixty-one tickets before that elephant got hold of me."

Mattywill sniffed and scooted closer so as not to be heard. "Abel and I sold all of ours and went back and got more. Folks felt sorry for us because we were your kin, so they bought tickets. We sold plenty on account of your being out there. Oh, I bet you thought you were really something sitting out there on that elephant, didn't you, with folks worrying about you. You got to rest on that animal all afternoon while Abel and I worked. And now you're going to get to be Miss Columbia just because of that old elephant of yours!"

Stiff as I was, I leapt to my feet with a chicken leg in one hand and a sandwich in the other. "Mattywill, I want to talk to you alone. Come on over there by that cottonwood tree."

My cousin's eyes were coals of fire in the sunset. "I don't want to," she said, tossing her head.

Uncle Luke ordered her, "Go with Bethany if she wants to talk to you."

"All right," Pa. Stiff-legged, Mattywill walked through the high grass to a spot where there were no other folks to hear us.

Eating, I followed right after her. I didn't ask her, I told her. "You didn't care about me being out there scared to death at all, did you?"

She moved her shoulders. "The circus man who trains the elephants said they're as tame as our barn cats. That big old elephant wouldn't ever have hurt you. She wouldn't squash a bug if she knew she was doin' it."

"Not squash a bug? She could have rolled in the water and squashed me, forgetting I was on her back!" Right then I was so mad, I longed to jab my cousin with the end of the chicken leg.

"Oh, Bethany, she wouldn't have. He said kids take rides

on her back all the time. She never dumps 'em off."

"Well, *I* didn't know that, Mattywill Morris! She doesn't give 'em rides in lakes, I bet. I can't swim. I know you can, though. I wish it had been you out there in the lake on that animal instead of me. If it had been, I wouldn't have gone out selling tickets—not even if it was for our church, not while you were suffering from thirstiness and hungriness and just plain scaredness."

"What're you complainin' about, Bethany?" she asked me. "It's over now, ain't it, and you ain't no worse for it, are you?"

Between my clenched teeth I told her, "Yes, I am. I'm wet halfway up to my midsection, and I'm cold, and my heart's still going too fast."

"Oh, my, we're sure a cry-baby mawmouth, ain't we?"

My cousin was making fun of my unhappiness. It was that old green-eyed monster for sure. I said, "You're *jealous!* Envy's a sin, a bad one."

"I ain't jealous!"

"Yes, you are, and I think I know why. It's because I'm a better reader than you are, and because a lot of folks noticed me out in the lake, and because I got chosen to be the Gem of the Ocean. I don't want to be crowned, and I didn't want to be picked up by that elephant."

Mattywill was poison-sweet now. "And you got to be a angel in the Christmas pageant in Blue Fork last year. You come here to Prineville, where I've lived all my life, and right off folks start to be more interested in you than in me.

Folks I've known ever since I was Billy Bob's age know your name better'n mine because of them cussed elephants. And now you'll be Miss Columbia, the first one my town ever has. It ought to be me, not you."

"I wish it *was* you, Mattywill, and like I said, I wish it had been you out in Boone Lake, too, not me."

"I just bet you want me to be the Gem of the Ocean!" she said sarcastically, and then, quick as a rabbit, ducked around the other side of the tree.

I didn't follow her. While I ate my sandwich I felt the anger bubbling up yeastily inside me. I hoped I wouldn't be punished with a stomachache, I was eating so fast. Here I was with no mama at all and no pa anywheres near, and she was jealous. Well, *let her be*!

If I was to be the first Gem of the Ocean, I'd try to enjoy it. Why not? I'd earned it, hadn't I? Except for seeing the circus, I hadn't had any other good times all day. Selling tickets wasn't fun—I had hated asking strangers for money.

I went slowly back to where Aunt Reva and the others were and sat down. Before anyone said a word, I told them, "I don't want to talk, please—just eat. I have to get my strength up to be crowned. Right now I feel sort of wobbly on my legs."

Aunt Reva asked, "Did Mattywill comfort you? Where is she?"

"I don't know. Last I saw of her she was still at the tree. I bet she went to look at the rodeo horses again. She'll be back here later on."

"That's probably it," agreed my aunt. "She dotes on those horses, and what with all of the ticket selling, she didn't get to see the rodeo."

A half hour after I'd eaten, Mayor Cass and the sheriff came to fetch me. I have to admit I felt sort of silly, walking in between them hand in hand while the band played "Beautiful Dreamer." We threaded our way around blankets and quilts, and as we went by, people clapped. I heard some whispering, too, about the "preacher's little girl."

The two men led me up onto the lantern-edged platform and sat me down in a chair where I could look out on all the folks below us. A lot of people had brought lanterns from home and had lit them and put them on their blankets. I couldn't spy Aunt Reva and Uncle Luke's blanket, so I couldn't tell if Mattywill had come back or not. Maybe she intended to stay with the rodeo horses and not see me get crowned at all.

Finally the band stopped playing, and Mayor Cass shouted, "First things first, folks. We'll have the crowning after I make a announcement. All the leftover tickets for the baby contest have been counted now. The fewest ones left are the red ones, the ones for Billy Bob Morris. It was a fair-and-square contest. Every baby started with the same number of tickets. Billy Bob'll be the Baby Jesus next Christmas!"

A lot of folks cheered until Mayor Cass yelled again, "Purely by accident and because she's got more grit in her little finger than a lot of folks do in their whole bodies, Billy Bob's cousin, Bethany Brant, will be Prineville's first Miss Columbia, the Gem of the Ocean. She's the daughter of our new town preacher we sold the tickets for. She showed her grit by stickin' with that elephant and never once lettin' out a scream or a whimper or a peep. She deserves our crown. Strike up the band, boys. Give us 'Columbia, the Gem of the Ocean.' "

When they started that tune, Mayor Cass pulled me to my feet and took off my sunbonnet while Deacon Cass plunked a long piece of red cloth over my shoulders. It smelled bad of camphor to keep out moths, but I didn't care. I was still damp from the lake and it made me warmer.

While I stood covered from shoulder to foot, the mayor took a silver-colored crown with sharp points all over its top out of a hatbox. He held it over my head and then slowly set it down onto me.

It was too big. It slid down over my forehead toward my nose. The mayor whispered to me, "Pull out your ears as far as you can or bunch up your hair."

I couldn't pull out my ears, so I gathered up my long curls as best as I could and stuffed them under the crown to stop it from slipping.

I said, "Thank you, Mister Mayor," and went back to sit down.

After the crowning came speeches from the men on the platform. Then, finally, came the fireworks set off from a raft in the lake. We all turned our chairs around to watch the showers of green, orange, white, yellow, and red lights. They were pretty, though I was getting so weary, I had a hard time keeping my eyes open.

I couldn't truly say that I enjoyed being the Gem of the Ocean, although it spited Mattywill. I was just sorry things were the way they were between us. Right now I wanted Pa with me again—even if he and Abel and I had to live in a tent on the prairie.

I cheered up a bit when Mayor Cass came to take my crown off my head—because it was heavy. I cheered up even more when he said to me, "Little gal, I just had a note sent up to me. Two of the saloon keepers here admired your grit so much that when they found out you was the minister's girl, they donated fifty dollars each toward the new church."

A whole hundred dollars! I'd earned that by acting brave. I looked up at the stars and I thanked the Lord for blessing me.

৯ 7 ৯

NOT MUCH
TO COMFORT
ANYBODY

That night when I slid down wearily between my quilts I
hoped to fall asleep right off. I didn't, though. As I lay there
listening to Mattywill's deep breathing, I felt something
move along the side of my foot! Frog warts, what was it?
And what should I do about it—jump out of bed yelling for
help or stay quiet so as not to rile whatever it was? Or toss
off the quilt on top of me real fast and roll over out of bed?

After a little bit of thinking I threw back the bedding. By
the moonlight pouring in through the window I could see
what was in bed with me. A horned toad. Just a plain ordinary everyday horned toad. Ugly-looking and scaly and dry,
but it couldn't hurt me. Being from Texas, I knew about

most of its wild critters. I knew, too, how it got inside my bed. Mattywill had put it there. She'd gotten hold of a horned toad and put him in my bed to scare me. She wanted me to yelp and run. I'd bet she was only pretending to be asleep.

Well, danged if I'd satisfy her. I decided to be quiet, like I hadn't noticed anything at all. Let her think I'd plunked myself down on the critter and squashed him flat, although I was glad I hadn't. He hadn't done me any hurt.

While I reached down and got hold of the toad, I was figuring what I'd be doing next. I put him into the pillowcase I took off my pillow. I had thought of a plan for him.

Finally, after a long time, Mattywill got up and went outside. This was what I'd been waiting for. Quick as a flash, I went over to her bed with the pillowcase and shook Mr. Horned Toad between her quilts way down at the bottom. He was her bedfellow now!

When she came back, I waited to see what would happen. But she didn't do anything at all. For all I knew, she slept all night long with that critter, because there was nary a peep out of her all the time I was awake. She was sure a tough customer, but so was I. We were a match for one another. I figured now that a war had started between us. I hoped it would be a short one, because it was going to be fought in territory she knew better than I did.

The rest of that summer was quiet—not the peaceful kind but the stone-dead silence that shouted at you. We didn't talk to each other, and we didn't look at each other, either. I couldn't forgive what she'd said to me, and she couldn't forget that Prineville people thought I had been a girl heroine.

Before long my aunt took notice that Mattywill and I weren't friendly. I knew she talked to Mattywill about it because Aunt Reva told me so one day late in July when we were alone together in the kitchen. I was ironing aprons in the summer heat.

As she rocked in the chair nursing Billy Bob, my aunt said to me, "Bethany, you and Mattywill don't seem to get along very well these days. She says she keeps out of your way because you're so hard to get along with."

Me, hard to get along with? I pushed the flatiron down so hard, I nearly scorched the apron on the board. It wasn't me. I hadn't started the trouble. I wished I could yell out that it was all Mattywill's doing, but I knew I'd better not. I had to remember all the time that Abel and I were guests here, not even paying ones, and I was a preacher's daughter, meek and mild.

Instead I said, "Mattywill doesn't take to me teaching her, Aunt Reva. Maybe it'd have gone better if I was a mite older than she is."

"Probably so, Bethany. How is Mattywill progressing?"

I wished there was something truly good I could say to that question, but Mattywill wasn't up to snuff in either her reading or her spelling. I was able to say, "Well, she shows some real hope when it comes to arithmetic."

"Do you think she'll qualify to be a sixth-grader?"

"I sure do hope so. If she doesn't, it won't be for my lack of trying to get her up to the point where I am in school."

"I know you do try, Bethany." Aunt Reva sighed. "I know. I hear you teaching her night after night. You're a good girl. It can't be altogether pleasant for you here with your mother gone and your father traveling for months and you being used to a town and having your own house to live in."

Hearing these things, and knowing they were all true, made me feel like bawling out loud, but I bit my lip and went on ironing. I did say, "I'm glad to help you, Aunt Reva. I'll be honest with you. I'd rather be in a nice cool barn or out under a cottonwood by a creek than in the kitchen ironing beside a hot stove." As I put the heavy iron into the metal holder on the stove to fold the apron, I went on. "But Pa isn't having it so good, either. Being a preacher on horseback isn't easy. Last time he wrote, he said he rode ninety miles from one place to another and had got shot at once because somebody wanted his horse and saddle. He'd had to gallop to put distance between him and the robber."

"Yes, you read us that dreadful letter. The Lord looked after him. Well, he'll be home in October before the real snows start. That's only three months from now."

I knew—I was counting the weeks.

Aunt Reva went on. "Mattywill has been an only child for a long time, Bethany, and has never gone to school. She hasn't been around many children her own age. She hasn't had it so easy, either, you know. I've been trying to tell her how to behave herself at school."

I nodded. What she was trying to say was that Mattywill didn't know how to share. Well, that sure was the truth. Too bad she didn't seem to catch on to her ma's teaching her manners any better than she did to my teaching her reading.

The middle of August, Billy Bob got sort of sick, crying a lot and spitting up what he ate. The roses faded some from his cheeks, too. After one long night of his nonstop bawling, Aunt Reva asked Uncle Luke to hitch the team and take her to town to see the doctor. Because I was good with Billy Bob, she asked me to go along. Sometimes when I sang to him, he'd go to sleep even faster than for her. Mattywill didn't have any idea of how to handle her baby brother. She grabbed him like a sack of beans whenever she picked him up, instead of holding his head to steady him.

Mattywill wasn't asked to go with us, and she was miffed that I was. As I was getting into the wagon she whispered, so her ma couldn't hear, "I suppose you're gonna hear all over again how brave you are and how pretty and what a good Gem of the Ocean you made."

Preacher's daughter or not, I couldn't help saying, "Yes, siree. I'd like to hear something nice and pleasant said to me for a change." That fixed her.

So I went to Prineville that blistering hot August day,

sitting on the wagon seat between Aunt Reva and Uncle Luke. I held tightly onto Billy Bob, who thrashed about a lot, trying to kick off the cool sheet I had around him.

While Aunt Reva was at the doctor's with him and Uncle Luke was at the General Store, I had time to sashay a bit around town. Nobody seemed to remember me as Miss Columbia, although I'd never confess it to Mattywill.

I saw Deacon Cass, but I never got close enough to ask him about the collecting for our church and manse. He was never alone. The first time I spotted him, he was outside of a saloon with his pa and some other men. While I was standing pondering whether to go up to him or not, they went inside. I sat down on the boardwalk across the street, waiting for him to come out again.

He came outside alone, and I got up to run over. But before I could, a lady who'd been looking at bonnets in a store window came walking over to him.

I thought she looked a little bit like Mama, and this gave me a sharp pang. She was pretty, white-skinned and dark-haired, and dressed in a soft gray-and-white suit and carried a sunshade parasol.

Oh, how Deacon Cass slobbered over her! His hat nearly touched the ground as he whipped it off and bowed. I heard his voice say loudly, "Well, hello, Miss Penny. What a nice surprise to see you again so soon. How do you like our fair city so far?"

The minute I heard her voice, I knew who she had to

be—our new schoolteacher. What she did for a living was in her voice, the way it was in a lot of teachers' voices back in Blue Fork. It carried, just like a school bell. She said, "It's very warm, Mr. Cass, but no warmer than in Dallas. I hope it will cool off before school starts. It's not easy to cope with children suffering in the heat."

"Yes, Miss Penny, you're right about that. I imagine all the town bachelors wish they were school kids again."

"Oh, I doubt that, Mr. Cass."

"I sure do—for one."

I was disgusted with him. He wasn't only a saloon lizard, he was also a soft soaper. Why wasn't he collecting for Pa instead of sparking the new teacher?

I was still glaring at him when suddenly I heard my name called. It was Uncle Luke, waving at me from the porch of the General Store. He needed me. Still looking back over my shoulder at Deacon Cass, I went over to help my uncle carry out some of the parcels.

Inside the emporium I asked him, "Do you know if that Deacon Cass is still collecting for our church?"

One of the store clerks answered me. "He sure is. He put the bite on me last week."

I said, "That's good news."

"Well, I didn't have anything in my pockets to give him but twenty-five cents. Payday was next day."

That wasn't good news, so I kept quiet. Aunt Reva came out of the doctor's office a little bit later, and I was glad to hear that Billy Bob was only colicky and starting to teethe. The doctor gave her some medicine that would help the teeth come through easier. When Aunt Reva tried it on him later, it seemed to work just fine, thank the Lord.

Hot August finally petered to an end, and I was glad. School would be starting real soon now, and was I ever looking forward to it. I wanted to see some girls' faces besides Mattywill's sour one. Abel was, too. He was bored with seeing only grown-up menfolk for so many months, and he wanted to be with other boys.

As the month went by, though, Mattywill got more and more sour. Part of that was on account of me and the lessons that never stopped. The other part was that she had to wear dresses to school, and she didn't like the ones Aunt Reva had cut down for her out of her own clothes.

Well, school finally started in September, and off we went with lard-pail lunches of corn bread, boiled eggs, doughnuts, and fried chicken tied to our saddles. Abel towed my no-good horse behind his own to get me there in time. Otherwise I never would have made it.

Right off Abel and I took to Miss Penny. Because this was the first class ever held in our brand-new schoolhouse, Miss Penny had to figure out where all of the kids she was meeting for the first time belonged by grade. She decided after having them read out loud one at a time and do arithmetic problems at the blackboard. Because Abel and I had always gone to school, we did just fine and got assigned to fourth- and sixth-grade books.

Miss Penny was pleased with Abel and me and told us, "I see that you Brants have had a lot of schooling. I may ask you two to help the others less lucky than you—particularly you, Bethany."

Hearing this made my heart fall. I could feel Mattywill's dark eyes boring into my back because I'd already gotten a compliment from the teacher. My cousin hadn't done as well as Abel and I had. Even if she had done long division, fractions, and decimals fine at the board, she couldn't read sixth-grade stuff without falling over the words. So I hadn't brought her up all the way to me the way Aunt Reva had wanted! I'd failed. Aunt Reva wouldn't be mad at me because she'd know I'd done my best. But I knew this would be another thing Mattywill would have against me.

Mattywill's weren't the only eyes boring into me. There were Mack eyes, too—two seven-year-old boy twins, and two girls nearer my age named Arletta and Fairy Fay. They were Macks, all right, redheaded and red-faced like their ma and their baby brother. I could tell right off that they just hated us Morrises and Brants because Billy Bob had won the baby contest at the Fourth of July celebration. Every time I turned around, I'd see a Mack watching me, sticking out a tongue. Pretty soon I got to sticking mine out, too. With my back turned, Miss Penny couldn't see me.

I figured one or two of the Macks might come over and say something bad to Abel and me while we ate our lunch under a tree, but it was Mattywill who came. She stood over me and said, "You didn't do so dandy as a teacher, Bethany."

Here it came! But I had my answer all ready. "As a student, Mattywill, you didn't work as hard as you should have. That's why you got put in the fifth grade. Don't you blame me for that." This was the truth, and sometimes bitter truths just had to be said.

"I hate you, Bethany," she snapped, then went to sit alone on the schoolhouse steps and eat her lunch.

What an ugly word *hate* was! Pa said it was uglier than cuss words. I'd never had it said to me before, and it stuck in my hide like a burr. I knew it would leave an ache in me for a long time.

Abel told me, "Mattywill's jealous of you, Bethany."

"What for, Abel? She's got a ma and a pa at home and a house of her own and a baby brother. She's . . ."

I would have gone on, but just at that moment the girl who shared a desk with me came over and plunked herself down beside me. She had wild-looking, black curly hair and black eyes, and she wore a tattered pink gingham dress, boys' shoes, and no stockings. She scratched at a bare leg as she introduced herself. "I'm Callie Stark. My pa works at The Dutchman Saloon. He's a bartender. You're the elephant rider, ain't ya? The Mack kids told me all about you and that other girl who came to school with you."

"We're Bethany and Abel Brant, and we know about the Macks."

Callie nodded. "Arletta Mack—she's the one who's our age—she says your pa's a preacher."

"That's right. He's off circuit-riding right now."

Callie went on. "I haven't got a ma anymore. She's dead. Is your ma dead, too? I can see you both got on black arm bands, and I know what that means. I've lived in lots of places in Texas and went to school in every one of 'em. That's why I'm up with you in the sixth grade. Where'd you go to school?"

Callie Stark could sure ask questions fast. I told her, "Our mama's dead. We lived in Blue Fork before we came here."

Counting on her fingers, Callie said, "I've been to school in Amarillo and Fort Worth and Dallas and Abilene. I like to read, and I like poetry. Do you?"

Before I could say a word, she went into:

"Come on then, my dearest dear
And present me to your pa
For I know you've got tobaccer
And I'm bound to have a chaw."

When I said it was pretty, though I didn't mean it, she went on, "I learned that one in a place that didn't have a jail, so they put my pa, who was a gambler then, in a dry well fifteen feet deep. They kept him there overnight till

92

they ran us both out of town the next morning. I sat down by that well and sang 'Nellie Gray' and 'White Wings' and 'Beautiful Mabel Clare' and 'Kitty Wells,' and recited poetry all night long to hearten him."

Abel said, "That was kindly of you, Callie."

"I thought so, too, Abel. Do you play card games and shoot dice? I do."

He answered her fast. "Nope, not with Pa being a preacher."

She laughed. "I don't know much about preachers. But I do know that everybody ought to at least know how to play poker. Say, who's that other gal who came with you this morning, the sour one over there on the steps who looks like she lives on pickle juice?"

I explained. "That's Mattywill Morris, our cousin. We're living with her folks till the townfolks can build a church and house for us to live in. Mattywill hates school."

Abel said, "And just now she told Bethany that she hates her."

"Hmmm." Callie looked at me. "How come?"

"She wanted to be the Gem of the Ocean on the Fourth of July and I got picked instead. Plus I had to teach her all spring and summer, and she didn't cotton to it."

"Who made you do that?"

"Pa and Uncle Luke and Aunt Reva."

"Grown-ups, huh? Why didn't you say no? I would have."

I sighed. Callie Stark sure didn't know anything about

being a minister's daughter. I figured from what she'd said and how she looked that bartenders' kids got to run wild. Lucky Callie!

"You're gonna be Miss Penny's teacher's pet, Bethany. I know it. I can tell. You'll be her monitor, and I bet you get to clap the erasers outside to clean 'em. I've met so many schoolmarms by now that I know their earmarks."

Once more I let out a sigh. That would be just dandy. It would make more bad feeling between Mattywill and me. Well, I knew a thing or two, also. Sulking around the way she was now, she wouldn't have any friends at school. Danged if I'd tell that to her, though. She ought to have enough brains to figure out that there were four Macks to three of us, and we ought to stick together at least at school. Split up, it would only make things harder for us.

I was beginning to like Callie and wanted her for a friend. I could sure use one. I decided to tell her about our troubles. I asked her, "Do you know Deacon Cass, the mayor's son?"

"Who don't? He comes into the Dutchman all the time for his beer and red-eye."

"Callie, does he collect money in there to build our church?"

"Sometimes he does. Pa says when he feels like it, he gives him some money. Pa says he's a pest."

I told her, "He's supposed to be money raising for the church full-time, but I have the feeling that he isn't keeping his mind on his business."

Callie giggled. "If you ask me, he hasn't got much mind. Right now he's sweet on Miss Penny, and that's all that's in his head. She's living at lawyer Templeton's house for September. Then she'll go to live with Mayor Cass and his wife for a month."

I knew how teachers boarded first one place, then another. I didn't know how Miss Penny felt about it, but I doubted that I'd like living under the same roof with Deacon Cass. It'd be worse knowing he felt mushy about me.

As I let out my deepest sigh of all, Callie grabbed me about the shoulder and rested her head next to mine. Then she snuggled her head up to Abel's and held him fast for a minute, too. How friendly this girl was! My brother and I had been lucky. We'd made a good friend the very first day of school. While other kids ran around on the schoolgrounds playing cowboys and Indians or chasing each other in tag, Callie had come to sit down with us and had given us her friendship.

When I got home from school that night, I learned that Callie had given me something else besides her friendship. Lice!

Abel didn't get 'em because he didn't sit next to her all day. Oh, how Mattywill loved my getting lice. She laughed while Aunt Reva parted my hair over and over and doused my scalp with stinging kerosene, killing the little gray-white bugs.

My cousin asked me, "Are you going to write your pa

about your lice, Bethany? Are you still going to keep on bein' friends with that black-headed gal at school?"

I told her fiercely, "Yes, I am. We're getting rid of the lice. Pa wants me to make friends with other town kids, and Callie's nice. I'll get her a bottle of kerosene as a friendship present. I've got enough money for that."

"Girls, girls!" scolded Aunt Reva. "Bethany, I'll give you some kerosene for your friend. Mattywill, this isn't one bit funny. Go to the barn and do something useful out there."

❈ 8 ❈

HAPPY BIRTHDAY?

I rode to school the next morning with a bottle of kerosene tucked in the deep pocket of my pinafore, and before school started, I gave it to Callie. After riding on my poky horse with it sloshing around, I was glad to get rid of it. I told Callie quietly, "This is for those things you've got on your head. It'll get rid of 'em. It makes your scalp sore, but all you have to do is comb it through your hair."

She scratched her head. "Oh, are they back again?"

"Yes, they are."

"Thank you kindly, Bethany," she said, and put the bottle in her dress pocket. "I'll use it tonight."

The rest of that morning at school went like the day before. The way Mattywill acted would see to it that she wouldn't make many friends there. She never once smiled at anybody. She drummed her fingers on her desk when others were reading out loud. She yawned. She almost snarled out loud when Abel and I recited, and she glared over and over at me like a thunderhead ready to open up and pour down rain. Once when Fairy Fay Mack made a mistake in a multiplication problem at the blackboard, she laughed loudly. Miss Penny rapped on her desk with her ruler and said sharply, "Be quiet. I do not permit rudeness in my classroom, Mattywill Morris!" Hearing that took some of the stuffing out of my cousin because everybody in the room turned around and stared at her. She had sat there and turned red with shame while the four Macks grinned wickedly at her being embarrassed.

Real late that morning I got hit hard in the back of the head by a spitball. Who fired it? A Mack or Mattywill? No, I wouldn't give the kid who threw it pleasure by turning around to look, even if the thing had hurt. I stared straight ahead at Miss Penny, even though I wasn't listening to a word she said.

At noon I couldn't figure why Miss Penny announced that she wanted to talk with me alone at lunchtime. Scared, I racked my brain but couldn't figure out what I'd done that was wrong. All the same, I was twitching as I stood in front of her desk when all the other kids had left the schoolhouse.

She got right to the point. "Bethany, I have noticed that you, your brother, and Mattywill seem to be disliked by the Mack children. I've seen them sticking out their tongues at you three."

I might have known she'd spotted that. Teachers saw everything!

All I said was "Yes'm, we are."

"Would you mind telling me why?"

"It's about Jesus, ma'am."

"Jesus?" She looked amazed.

"Yes'm. Baby Mack's family wants him to be Baby Jesus in the Christmas pageant. We all want our baby, Billy Bob, to get the job. Billy Bob had the most tickets bought in his name at the Fourth of July picnic, so he's going to be it."

"My word, ticket selling?" Miss Penny looked upset. "It's a strange way to get a part in a holy pageant."

I nodded. "It doesn't suit me too well, either. They could have drawn straws." I added, "Deacon Cass was the one who arranged for selling the tickets." I figured that would put a spoke in his wheel with Miss Penny.

"Did he, now? What will this money be used for?"

"For buying lumber for a church. Pa's a preacher. It'll be his church. Until it and a manse get built, Abel and I have to stay with our kinfolks, Mattywill's pa and ma."

The teacher nodded. "So, that explains why you three come to school on horseback. Well, at least the tickets were sold for a good cause."

I liked her and went on to tell her more about my family.

"Mattywill's folks wanted her to be in the sixth grade like me, so I've been teaching her for months now—every night after supper. But I'm not a real teacher like you."

Miss Penny smiled up at me. "So, you want to be a teacher, Bethany?"

"No, not anymore, ma'am."

"I think I see what you may mean. Mattywill didn't like being taught, eh? A recalcitrant pupil is a difficult chore."

"What does that big word mean?"

"The dictionary is over there. Look it up. *Recalcitrant* spells the way it sounds. Make a friend of the dictionary the way you seem to be doing with Callie Stark. By the way, I saw you give her a bottle today before school started. I trust it was kerosene. It looked like it."

"Yes, ma'am, it was." She saw *everything*—even me handing the kerosene to Callie, and thinking I was doing it secretly.

Miss Penny said, "I'm glad you gave it to her. Otherwise I would have had to call her father in. I'm glad you took to Callie, but I'm afraid you may find some of the other boys and girls here are on the side of the Mack children. They've had most of the summer to turn youngsters against you Morrises and Brants."

I told her, "We don't care. We don't come to town much except for school."

Miss Penny was done with me now. She told me, "I'm sorry about the Macks' attitude, Bethany. I'll speak to them after school today, and if that doesn't work, I'll speak to their parents. What I ask of you is that you don't make any trouble by starting a fight with them here at school."

"I'll do the best I can to keep out of their way. But I sure hope you can stop whoever threw that spitball at me this morning. It hurt."

"Your cousin did that. I saw her. But I thought it would be better if I sent her home with a note for her mother rather than discipline her with the ruler."

This made me nod. Yes, Aunt Reva would tear into Mattywill. But how did Mattywill learn to make a spitball when she'd never gone to school before?

Miss Penny asked me one last question. "When will your father be coming home, Bethany?"

"Late October."

"Good. I see from your school records that you and Abel have no mother?"

"No, ma'am, not since the first of the year. That's why we wear these arm bands. Aunt Reva's mighty kind to us, though."

Before I went outside, I looked up *recalcitrant*. It came out to be "I don't want to," which ought to be Mattywill's motto these days. Well, Aunt Reva would fix her wagon!

That very night, though, I changed my mind a bit about Aunt Reva. When she opened the note Miss Penny had given Mattywill for her, she looked quite stern. I'd had high hopes that Mattywill might get the thrashing she deserved.

But Aunt Reva stuck up for her own daughter in the end. She asked, "Did you throw a spitball at Bethany, Mattywill?"

Like a cat at the cream jug, my cousin grinned, and said sweetly, "Well, Ma, I made one. I saw a kid do it yesterday. I aimed it at Fairy Fay Mack, but I missed."

Abel, who'd heard this, cried out, "Fairy Fay sits way across the room from Bethany."

"Ma, my aim was way off," Mattywill protested. "I never threw a spitball before. What do you expect?"

"I expect you to throw no more, that's what I expect. That's all I have to say on this. I'll write a note for you to take to your teacher tomorrow."

Oh, that big old liar, Mattywill! How I longed to crown her—and not with the Gem of the Ocean crown, either, but with the full water pitcher at Aunt Reva's elbow. That wouldn't have been a Christian act, but it sure would have been satisfying. Mama wouldn't have let me off so easy if I'd thrown a spitball! Frog warts!

School went on for another seven weeks with me becoming more and more friendly with Callie and less and less friendly with the Macks and Mattywill. My cousin finally made a friend, a skinny little freckly girl named Maudine, who never spoke to anyone but who followed Mattywill around like her shadow. Abel made a friend, too, named Jonadab Fenstermaker.

Though I didn't see hide nor hair of Deacon Cass or the mayor in those weeks, I did learn from Callie that Deacon was still working at collecting money for our good cause. Her pa told her he saw him plenty, but he didn't have any idea how much Deacon had collected.

One day in the first part of October I caught Deacon Cass all alone. That was only by accident because Miss Penny had sent me on an errand to the General Store. She wanted me to buy blacking for the school stove since it was now getting cold enough to light it.

He was just coming out as I was going in. I nabbed him on the walk and asked, "How's the collecting going for the church and manse?"

"Not too bad, little girl." He peered hard at me. "Ain't I seen you before? Ain't you the Gem of the Ocean girl?"

"Yes, that's me, but that was last July. Will you have all the money you need by the time Pa comes home?"

"Who's Pa?"

"My father, Preacher Brant."

"Oh, yeah. I hope to have quite a tidy sum before long, kiddie. When's he coming home?"

"Late this month. He's out circuit-riding because he hasn't got a church here."

"No, I won't have all of it by then. I can tell you that right now."

He exasperated me mightily. He hadn't recognized me

right off without peering and blinking; he reminded me of things I'd like to forget; and he called me "kiddie." His eyes weren't on me the way they ought to be, but on a pretty lady who had just sashayed past us into the store.

I got his attention back by saying, "We're counting on you to get us a church and a manse."

He laughed at me. "I suppose you want a mansion, huh?"

This got my goat. "No, sir, just an ordinary house but bigger'n a henhouse. That's all we want. If Pa was here, he'd collect, too, but he isn't. And when he is in this part of the county he's generally miles out of town on Uncle Luke's ranch. We aren't begging."

He chuckled now. "Don't you fret, kiddie. Leave it to me. I'm usually on the job collecting. I don't have to have your papa's help. That's about all I do these days—fund-raisin'."

I couldn't help but ask, "What'll you do when this is over?"

"I'll find something else, I reckon. What's it to you?"

"It isn't anything to me once we get a church and a roof over our heads. And the sooner the better, please."

Now he gave me a mean look and said, "I've got four sisters older'n me. You sound just like 'em, snapping out orders."

"I'm not giving you any orders, Mr. Cass."

"No, but by the tone of your voice you'd sure like to, wouldn't you, sis? Well, let me tell you, I don't take no orders from anything that wears petticoats."

I couldn't help but say, "From the tone of your voice, you don't take orders from anybody. If I was a grown-up lady, I sure wouldn't take to the likes of you."

At that I stuck my nose up into the air and sailed right past him to get the stove blacking. Though Deacon was a good-for-nothing galoot, I figured I'd better leave off talking to him before I lost my temper and got him mad. If he stopped collecting for us, there'd be no one else to do it, and we'd never get our church. Oh, but Deacon the man was turning out to be just as slow a mover as Deacon the horse.

Late one Saturday afternoon toward the end of the month, Pa came riding home. At first Abel and I didn't even know him. He'd grown a yellow beard and he had a different horse from the one he'd started out riding. The new one was a pinto, as good an animal as the first one.

Once we recognized who it was, Abel and I ran to him, both of us crying. We were so glad to see him again. Oh, how I'd missed him! I kept dreaming over and over about being back home in Blue Fork, happy with him and Mama again. I hated to wake up. It was terrible to feel like an orphan for so many months. I hung on to his stirrup and held my cheek against his boot until he told me, "Hey, let go, Bethany! Let me get off and go see Luke and Reva. Is everything all right here?"

I said, "Nobody's sick, Pa."

"That's good to hear."

When he dismounted, Abel and I bear-hugged him while

105

he hugged us. Then I asked, "Did you ride through Prine-ville?"

"No, I came in from another direction. Tell me, how's the church progressing?"

Hearing this made me sigh. I'd mentioned the church in all nine letters I'd written him, telling him each time that the lumber still hadn't arrived yet, so the church hadn't been built. Pa should have known this.

I said, "Pa, I wrote you nine letters. How many did you get?"

"Five. That's not bad for a man riding circuit."

"Well, Pa, in all of 'em I told you the church wasn't built yet. Did you get the one about Abel and me starting school?"

"Yes, that letter was the last one I got. There were bad hailstorms at some of the places I went these last weeks, so the mail could have come after I left and still be trailing me. It's slow going in storms. So the church isn't up yet? What about a house for us to live in?"

"There isn't anything at all up! The mayor's son is still collecting."

Abel put in, "But he sold lots and lots of tickets at the Fourth of July picnic so Billy Bob could be the Baby Jesus at Christmastime. That ticket money went toward the church."

Pa looked down at me. "You didn't write me that news, Bethany."

"No, I was scared to. I thought you wouldn't like it and

it'd upset you. I didn't tell you that I rode an elephant that same day either."

"An *elephant?*" Pa looked astonished.

"She sure did, Pa," Abel rattled on, "and she was the Gem of the Ocean that night because of it, and that made Mattywill sore as a boiled owl, and she's been sore ever since."

"Well, I see that I'd better have a long talk with Luke about all that's happening here," said Pa as he took the saddlebags off the pinto.

"Pa, the elephant didn't hurt me. Not much is happening. That's what's so bad about it." To change the subject I asked, "Where'd you get the pinto?"

"Luke's horse went lame last month, so I traded a man who could doctor it to health for this one. It's older than Luke's horse, but it's a good one. He won't feel cheated." Pa sighed.

From the expression on his face I could see that Pa felt cheated, himself, because he hadn't come home to a church and a manse. Well, so did I. I hoped Pa could stir Deacon Cass up now that he was home, but I doubted that he could.

Later, after all the family and cowboys had welcomed him, Pa and I talked outside on the veranda. It wasn't about the hard times he'd had on his circuit or the funerals, camp meetings, baptizings, and weddings he'd been busy with. He'd already told about those at the supper table.

We talked about how we both ached for Mama and

about Mattywill and me and all the trouble there was between us. It surprised him that she'd be so angry at me for nothing.

Finally he said, "That's too bad you and your cousin don't get along better."

"It isn't my fault, Pa, not the elephant, or Miss Columbia, or the teaching."

As he gathered me to his side he said, "You're a good girl, Bethany. I know you've tried, and it also appears to me that you've been tried sorely here."

"What'll I do, Pa?"

"Bear up under your burden until we move into town. Behave yourself. Your aunt needs you here. You're a big help to her, and a comfort, too. Abel and I haven't been much of that because we're men. I figure that it's been you who's earned us all our welcome here."

"But, Pa, it wears me down something terrible. Sometimes I think I'm going to blow up and smite Mattywill hip and thigh. She says she hates me."

"You'll have to be strong and patient with her. She doesn't mean that."

I longed to say, "Oh, yes, she truly does," but I didn't.

It was like him not to understand. Sometimes grown-ups either didn't see or they played blind—the way Aunt Reva had when it came to Mattywill and the spitball that had hit me. Pa didn't know how it was getting harder and harder for me to behave myself when Mattywill and the Mack kids and Deacon Cass didn't bother to behave themselves. It wasn't fair—not one bit.

I was right about Pa not being able to stir up Deacon Cass. When he and Uncle Luke went to see him and the mayor, they found out that so far Deacon had only two-thirds of the money that was needed. Pa told us what the mayor said when he and my uncle got back home.

Mayor Cass had agreed that it was true his son had been a bit lax lately. He was courting the new schoolmarm instead. And the mayor added that he didn't blame Deacon one bit for being smitten with Miss Penny's charms.

And that was that—that was his poor excuse for his poor excuse of a son!

November came in blustery with wind, and with it came a real peck of trouble. Mattywill and I were both born that month, she in the last part of it and I in the first.

On the second day of the month Aunt Reva called me out back to talk with me in private. She pressed two silver dollars into my hand and said, "Bethany, I want you to go to town with Luke this Saturday, when he goes to buy supplies. Buy some cloth for a new dress for Mattywill's birthday. Don't tell her what you're doin'. Bring the cloth and trim back here wrapped in brown paper, so she can't see it. I'll make her dress while she's at school. Will you do it?"

Buy cloth for *her*? Frog warts! What about my birthday,

two days from now? I wasn't keen to do this, but I agreed to please Aunt Reva. "What kind of cloth should I buy?"

"Cotton. It's to be a school dress. Calico or gingham. There's a big selection at the General Store these days, now that Christmas is coming. Pick something that you think will suit her."

So that Saturday I rode to Prineville in the wagon with a long list of things Aunt Reva needed and two dollars in the beaded reticule that had been Mama's.

Oh, how I looked over the bolts of cloth at the General Store! There was pink- and red- and blue- and green- and yellow-checkered ginghams, and calicoes of just about every color the rainbow had.

Finally I found just what I was looking for. I couldn't resist it. It was a dull, dark, purplish-blue calico print with brown-and-white flowers in it. That color would look terrible on somebody as dark as Mattywill—even worse than the mustard-brown and frog-green calicoes I'd fingered, too. I bought four yards of dark brown rickrack trim to go with it and had it all wrapped in brown paper the way Aunt Reva had wanted.

As we started for home Uncle Luke asked me, "Is that Mattywill's dress cloth there, Bethany?" and he nodded toward the package on my lap.

"You bet it is, Uncle Luke. It ought to suit her just dandy. I'll love watching her wear it."

I knew I hadn't behaved myself and should have felt guilty, but I sure felt better about things because I hadn't!

CHRISTMAS
IS
COMING!

I stood there while Aunt Reva unwrapped her parcel after supper. She looked at the cloth and rickrack trim a long time. Then she looked hard at me, but not one word did she say. She just wrapped up the package again and said, "Thank you, Bethany, for shopping for me."

I told her, "You've got forty-six cents in change coming to you."

"You keep it as a present for doing the chore."

"But I don't want it, Aunt Reva."

"I want you to have it as a memento of your shopping trip."

I could tell by the way she acted that she wasn't taken with what I'd picked out for Mattywill.

I kept hoping the day before my birthday and on my birthday that the Morrises would remember me the way they were remembering Mattywill. I didn't expect Pa to remember. He had plenty on his mind right now, and Abel was too little to think about any birthday but his own.

But nobody remembered me! Nobody said a word about it. Back in Blue Fork it'd been Mama who had done the remembering for all of us. She'd baked the birthday cakes and bought or made the presents.

That night in my bed I kept thinking about birthdays I'd had when Mama was alive. Usually she'd invite my friends from school over for cake and hand-cranked ice cream. Mama had told me to ask them weeks ahead of time. And this year there wasn't anything at all for me! The ache in my heart for Mama brought tears to my eyes, but I didn't cry out loud for fear that Mattywill would hear me and laugh at me as a mawmouth.

Not long after my birthday Mattywill went to town with her pa. I figured she had been so sore that I got to go that her ma had let her go this time. But, of course, I didn't ask her because we weren't speaking.

Then came November the fifteenth. To my surprise a big white whipped-cream cake was brought to the supper

112

table. Who was it for? It was too late for me and too early for Mattywill.

To my astonishment everybody sang, "Happy Birthday, dear Bethany." Then they all sang, "Happy Birthday, dear Mattywill."

I didn't understand what was happening. "My birthday's over," I told them.

Mattywill said, "Mine ain't till the thirtieth. How come there's a cake now?"

"Girls, we know," came from Aunt Reva. "This is a *combination* birthday party. It's for both of you together on the fifteenth, halfway through the month. Mattywill and Bethany, before I cut the cake, I have a gift for each of you."

I braced myself, waiting to see Mattywill's new dress. Aunt Reva brought it out, holding the flounced skirt as wide as she could. That didn't help prettify it one bit, though. It was the ugliest dress I had ever set eyes on.

Pa said, "Sort of dark, isn't it, Reva? It appears to me to be like an old lady's dress, not a young girl's."

Aunt Reva told everyone brightly, "Oh, no. Bethany chose it for Mattywill. I doubt that she agrees with you. She thinks it is very beautiful, don't you, Bethany?"

I gulped and nodded, looking at the cake, not the people.

After Aunt Reva had given the dress to her daughter she said, "And now for Bethany's birthday present."

Back she went to her bedroom, and she was out in a minute with dress number two. It was calico, too, and made from the same pattern. But it was a dull red-and-white print with dark red rickrack trim. The dress was terrible-looking, just about the worst color there was for a yellow-haired person like me. Frog warts!

I didn't have to ask who'd bought that cloth for me, but Aunt Reva told me all the same, "Bethany, dear, Mattywill chose this for you the day she went to Prineville." Then she sat down and asked, "Shall I cut the cake?"

"Sure," agreed Uncle Luke. He turned to Mattywill and me and asked, "Well, birthday gals, what do you think? Isn't this one of the best birthdays you've ever had?"

"Uh-huh, sure, Pa," came from Mattywill, sounding strangled.

I said, "Yes, Uncle Luke. I'll always remember it."

Aunt Reva was as cheerful as a robin. "I dare say neither of you will ever forget your birthday of 1899, will you, and each time you put on your lovely birthday dresses, you will be reminded. Naturally you'll be wearing them a great deal. They're for school, where all your classmates will see and admire you in them."

Oh, how sly grown-ups could be. Aunt Reva *knew* all along but never let on a word to me or Mattywill. I stole a glance at Pa and found him looking sort of mournfully at me. He knew, too, and I was sure Uncle Luke did also. The only one who didn't know was Abel, who had his mind fixed on the cake more than on us and the dresses.

I felt sick—both because I'd let my mean nature out and because it had come back on me, kicking me in the slats. Pa had said once that bad deeds and wicked thoughts had a way of doubling back on a body, and he'd been right. I didn't have much appetite for my piece of cake, good as it was. I looked at my cousin across the table from me. She was staring at me like she was measuring me with those black eyes of hers, wondering if I could really be evil enough to pull the same trick she had.

Now she knew that I was. Would this change her ways toward me?

It didn't. She wore her ugly dress to school the next day, and I wore mine. I told Callie the story of the birthday dresses, and she agreed that she'd never seen anything uglier than the colors of the two calicoes. When she asked me if I was sorry for what I'd done, I said straight out, "Not on your tintype, Callie Stark." And I wasn't, either!

November came slowly to an end. Some snow fell on the last day of the month, but not enough to keep us home. The horses could get through on the road, so we kept on attending, Mattywill trotting ahead and Abel towing my horse. The coming of colder weather hadn't made my horse any sprier. Even if I ran in front of him with a nose bag full of oats, I doubted that he had the yeast in him to trot faster to get at 'em.

By this time I'd given up the idea that we'd have a place of our own to live in or a church in 1899. By now it was too cold to put up any buildings. All over Prinevile there was lumber piled up under canvas covers waiting for springtime.

115

Each pile I saw gave me a pang because it reminded me that we'd be at Uncle Luke's for many more months.

Early in December, the preparations for the Christmas pageant started. I wasn't looking forward to it because I had the sinking feeling that I'd be expected to be a flying angel again, and I dreaded it.

At the first rehearsal in the General Store I learned that Pa would read the Bible verses for the pageant, and that Abel and Mattywill were to be shepherds. Billy Bob, of course, was the Baby Jesus, and Miss Penny was to be the Virgin Mary. Just as I feared, I'd been put down for the angel on ropes. I'd be flying from one end of the store's high balcony to the other end.

Mayor Cass picked the lanky sheriff to be Joseph and Callie and a boy from school to be more shepherds. No Macks were invited at all. As for animals, he planned to get real ones from the farms and ranches.

At the start of the rehearsal the town blacksmith measured me for the harness belt I would have to wear. He sure was a fast worker! Before the rehearsal was over that afternoon, he'd made a broad leather corset with a strong metal band in the middle and two loops on the front and back so I could do my flying. Later on he was going to paint it golden so that it would look better in public.

How I hated flying! I tried to get out of doing it that day, saying I couldn't because I was wearing a skirt; but the storekeeper brought me a boy's shirt and new stiff bib overalls to wear, so I had to go through with it.

I went up onto the balcony with the smith and his helper, and they threaded two ropes through my loops exactly the way this had been done in Blue Fork. I guess they make angels fly in Christmas pageants the same way all over the state.

Pa, the mayor, Abel, Mattywill, and everybody else stood below the high balcony staring up at me as I was let down on one of the ropes. It jerked me as I came to rest, and I tried not to kick my feet in a middle-of-the-air dance. Golly, it was a long way to the floor, but not so far that I couldn't see my cousin's scowl. She was jealous of this, too.

"That's fine, men," Pa shouted up to them. "Now, let's see her fly."

I sucked in my breath, thinking of my poor ribs, which were about to get an awful squeezing.

Because the blacksmith and his helper had never done this before, they seesawed me for a while, moving me from left to right, right to left. Finally they got the hang of it and I was able to grab hold of the rope and slide along it like I was flying. Later I'd be twitching my shoulders so that my muslin wings would flap a bit.

I didn't have to say my Bible speech about "good tidings" and "great joy" today because this was only practice, so I just swung back and forth, feeling the metal band pressing heavier and heavier on my ribs and waist. Nobody guessed how pained I was, least of all Mattywill Morris.

Thank heavens the angel part of the pageant wasn't long. I'd get hauled up out of the way the minute those shepherds below me heard what I had to say and skedaddled for Bethlehem.

At last I saw Pa motion to the shepherds. Then he yelled up to the men who had me in tow. "That's enough. Reel her in now."

I stopped swinging and tried to be stiff as I could while they slowly pulled me hand over hand up to the balcony railing.

"You look a mite pale. Are you all right, little girl?" the blacksmith asked me as he got me out of my harness.

"Sort of," I panted, holding my hands to my midsection.

He said, "Next rehearsal Gus and me'll do better. It's just that we never did this before. Angels are more in your pa's line of work than ours. Sorry if we hurt you."

I gave him a weak grin. I had such a stitch in my side that I couldn't say a word. I wouldn't say a word of complaint because it would make Pa feel bad. He'd been very proud of me when I flew in Blue Fork, and he wanted to be proud here, too.

After I climbed down from the balcony I went to sit beside the store's stove. As I warmed my sore sides I watched Mattywill, Abel, Callie, and the others milling around, being the shepherds at the manger. I couldn't help but be disgusted when I saw who was to be one of the three Wise Men. Deacon Cass. Him, a Wise Man? Nobody but his pa would ever think so. And, oh, the silly calflike way he looked at Miss Penny.

This was the first time Pa had ever met my teacher. They seemed to get along fine. I tried to hear if they talked about Abel and me, but it seemed to me that they never said anything that wasn't about the pageant.

After that first rehearsal the Mack kids were more ornery than ever in school. They stuck out their feet to trip my brother and me when we went to the blackboard.

That Friday, Abel got into a fight with both boy twins at once. Even if they were a year younger than he was, their being two didn't make it a fair fight. It happened at lunchtime. When Abel went down the school steps one Mack twin tripped him up on the middle step, and at the same time the other one threw himself onto my brother's back, so Abel went down into the cold mud. Over and over the three boys rolled, kicking and punching. Before long, they were so dirty that nobody could tell which was which.

I didn't know what to do, but I had to stop the fight. I would have tried to peel the nearest boy off, but Arletta Mack caught me by the hair, jerking me back. I felt helpless, twisting around trying to get away from her. She was stronger than she looked, and she had claw hands, too.

At the same time Fairy Fay Mack got hold of Mattywill, but she didn't fare so well as her sister. Out of the corner of one eye, I glimpsed Mattywill punch her in the face just like a boy would. Fairy Fay's nose started to bleed, so she ran off bawling and holding it.

119

It was Callie who stopped the boys' fight. She waded into the bundle of fists and feet and started pulling the three boys apart. Noble Callie! Seeing her do my job for me made me go wild. I booted Arletta backward in the shin, as hard as I could. When she let go of me to hop around, holding her leg, I ran over to help Callie. By now she was holding a muddy Mack at arm's length while he tried to sock her with his too-short arms.

"Get another boy!" she shouted at me.

I did. I reached down, grabbed hold of Abel, and pulled him up, panting and hitting the air with his fists. To keep him from hitting me I had to holler, "It's me, Bethany, your sister! Don't you hit me, Abel."

At that moment Miss Penny came running out of the schoolhouse. "What's happening here?" she cried.

Arletta answered her, "We were only funning, Miss Penny."

"Funning? It looks like fighting to me. What do you say, Callie?"

"Funning, Miss Penny," said Callie as she let go of her Mack.

"Who started this?" asked the teacher.

I looked at Arletta, who was glaring daggers at me. No, it'd be best if I kept what I knew to myself. I said, "Nobody, really. It just happened when Abel fell over one of the Mack boys on the step. I guess Abel accidentally stepped on his hand."

Abel said, "That wasn't what hap—"

"Hush, Abel," I warned him, and he hushed.

Now Miss Penny turned to my cousin. "What do you have to say, Mattywill?"

"Nothin', but it was fun like they told you."

Miss Penny sniffed. "Well, it does seem that nobody is about to admit or accuse anybody of anything here. Whatever you were doing, don't do it again, you hear?"

When she'd gone inside, Arletta told me fiercely, "That's just the beginning, Bethany Brant. You just wait and see."

I held my temper, but Mattywill didn't. "Try us one more time, Arletta, and you'll get what-for and be sorry," she said, flaring.

Arletta tossed her red head and walked off in the direction in which Fairy Fay and her brothers had gone.

Abel was wiping mud off himself and now went over to Mattywill. "I saw you punch Fairy Fay," he said. "You've got a good right fist for a girl."

"Yep, I sure do. Folks have to learn that they can't mess around with us at school."

Us? I caught at the word. Mattwill had used it two times. I'd never heard her say that before—just *I* and *me*. I wondered if her *us* included me, too. If it did, I didn't see or hear anything that would make me think so the rest of that school day.

That same day we had more trouble. When we went to

our horses after school was out, we found that our saddle girths had been cut. That meant we'd have to leave the saddles here and ride home bareback in the sleety weather.

I went in to tell Miss Penny about it, and she came out in the rain with a shawl over her head to look at them. She agreed a knife had been used on them.

I told her, "Uncle Luke or Pa will have to come with the wagon to fetch the saddles back to the ranch tomorrow."

"Yes, that's what will have to be done, all right. This is terrible, Bethany. Who would do such a thing?"

I didn't speak up, but Callie did. Standing beside the horses with Mattywill and Abel, she said, "It was one of the Macks. Arletta carries a pocketknife. I saw it on her."

"Did anybody see this happen?"

"The Macks are too smart for that," Callie replied.

Miss Penny took a deep breath. "Well, let's get those saddles into the schoolhouse till someone comes with a wagon for them."

Saddles are heavy and slippery when wet, but we got them to the schoolhouse through the mud. Then we rode home bareback, miserable and soaked and sore, too, from our horses' backbones.

Right off Mattywill told Uncle Luke and Pa about the cut girths.

Her pa exploded. "Cuss whoever'd do that! What're kids coming to nowadays? I hadn't planned to go to town tomorrow. I've got work to do here."

Pa volunteered. "I'll go for you, Luke."

"But you'll be going in to preach Sunday at the General Store."

"Two trips to town won't kill me after all the months I spent on horseback."

"All right, you take the team and wagon to the schoolhouse."

"Do any of you kids want to come?" asked Pa. Abel wanted to help Uncle Luke in the barn, and Aunt Reva made Mattywill stay and do her long reading assignment. But I was happy for the chance to be with Pa by my lonesome, so I said I wanted to go.

Pa smiled at me. "Then, it'll be just you and me, Bethany."

The next day Pa and I rode to Prineville, and we found Miss Penny waiting for us in the schoolhouse. She frowned while he carried the saddles to the wagon and covered them with a tarpaulin. When Pa came in to thank her for storing the saddles, I heard her tell him, "Reverend Brant, last night I made some inquiries here in town. It seems the Christmas pageant offends a number of people."

"Why are they offended, ma'am?"

She hesitated. "They put it rather inelegantly, I'm afraid, but they express it clearly. What they say is that you, a newcomer preacher, are not only narrating the pageant, but also your daughter is the angel in it and your son a shepherd. Your niece is also a shepherd and your nephew the

Infant Jesus Christ. What it comes down to is that the Brants and Morrises are 'hogging' the show."

"Hogging the show?" Pa looked surprised.

"Yes, Reverend." Miss Penny's lips were pressed together firmly. "There's more, I'm afraid."

"What would that be?"

"Certain people are saying that they will come to the pageant and will provide a distraction."

"What?"

"They will boo and hiss."

"Good Lord, would they?"

I spoke up now. "Sure, the Macks would. So would all their friends. They wanted their boy to be the Baby Jesus, but he didn't sell enough tickets. And there aren't any Macks at all in the pageant." I turned to my teacher and asked, "Miss Penny, did Mayor Cass ask any one of 'em to be in it?"

"No, he did not. I asked him that very question last night."

Pa was looking troubled, and now sat down on a bench. He thought for a time, then looked up at Miss Penny and said, "Yes, it isn't fair, is it? I should have noticed that, but I don't know the Mack family at all."

I said, "They cut our girths, Pa. I just know it was them."

Miss Penny added, "Very probably they did, Reverend."

Looking at his clasped hands, Pa sighed. "Unfortunately, I was out circuit-riding and didn't know about the baby contest. I would have stopped the ticket selling if I'd been around. And Deacon Cass can't return the money to those who bought a ticket in favor of the Mack baby because nobody could know all of them. But there is one thing I *can* do—even if Mayor Cass is against it."

"What would that be, Reverend Brant?"

"I can remove myself and my family from the pageant entirely—I mean, myself, Bethany, and Abel. I can't very well remove Mattywill and Billy Bob, who are not my immediate family—certainly not Billy Bob, because if I did that, I would offend the people who bought tickets for him."

Trying not to sound too happy, I asked, "Pa, I won't get to fly?"

"Not this year, Bethany. Maybe next year, though."

Oh, I wanted to turn cartwheels for joy but didn't dare.

Miss Penny said, "That could ease the tension a good deal. I'll talk to the mayor about replacing the children. But I do think he will want you to stay on as the narrator. You have a fine voice for it."

"Thank you, Miss Penny. That is up to the mayor. And thank you again for looking after the saddles."

After Pa left, I stayed behind just long enough to say, "Arletta Mack's got yellowish-red hair, and she's just about my size, so the angel harness would fit her fine. She'd make a dandy angel."

Miss Penny smiled. "That's very generous of you, Bethany. I'm sure Arletta and the Macks would like that very

125

much. It could make up somewhat for their baby not being in the pageant."

After having stuck that flea in her ear, I shut the schoolhouse door and splashed out to the wagon, wanting to whoop for happiness.

Though Arletta would learn how it felt to be an angel on ropes, I was sure she'd just love to have everybody's eyes on her, no matter how much it hurt. And I told myself that I wasn't really wishing her the badness that I had just gotten out of because her folks would be getting some joy out of it, too.

⤳ IO ⤶

TRUCES!

On the way home Pa stopped at the newly built town hall where the mayor had his office, and he and I trooped in together. Mayor Cass was in his office looking sleepy. So was Deacon Cass, sitting with his feet resting on his pa's desk. Though the mayor smiled, Deacon barely looked at me. He didn't have any use for people my age, just for pretty ladies like Miss Penny.

After Pa had refused the cigar the mayor offered, the older Cass asked, "What can I do for you, Reverend? Sit down, sir."

Pa sat down, but I stood because there wasn't another chair. My pa said, "I want my children taken out of the

Christmas pageant and other children put in their places. There's talk in town that we 'hog' the show. I'd like you to remove me as narrator, as well."

"Now hold your horses, Reverend." My father's words had made Mayor Cass wake up, and Deacon Cass hauled his feet off his pa's desk. "Reverend, you've got the best speaking voice around. You must stay in the show." Then the mayor turned to me. "How do you feel about not being an angel, honey?"

"All right, sir. I've already been the Gem of the Ocean this year. Make Arletta Mack the angel. And make another boy or girl a shepherd in my brother's place. He won't care. He's been a shepherd before."

Deacon Cass spoke up sharply. "Billy Bob Morris has got to stay in as the baby, though, because money's been spent on him."

"Yes, he does," agreed Pa.

"Reverend, I'd like you to narrate the show, and the Morris baby to stay on as the Baby Jesus."

"All right. I'll stay on." Pa got up, but before we left, he turned to Deacon and asked, "How's the collecting going for the church and manse?"

"Not so bad. There'll be a money tree at the pageant to pin paper money onto. And there'll be an iron pot beside it for the hard money. I figure on getting the rest of the money the night of the big show."

Pa spoke heavily now. "A money tree and a money pot at a Christmas pageant."

The mayor didn't understand what Pa meant at all. He boomed, "You bet. Ain't it wonderful—all the things my smart boy's dreamed up to get you your church and house, Reverend? No wonder he's a Wise Man in the show!"

I gulped, and I saw Pa swallow hard. All he said, though, was, "Yes, it's been remarkable, sir, simply remarkable the way God works his wonders here in Prineville. Come on, Bethany, we want to get started for home before the rain turns to sleet."

As we left, Mayor Cass called out, "See you next Saturday at the rehearsal."

"Yes, I'll be there."

I was quiet while we went to the wagon so as not to let my joy show. I was happy that Pa was still in the pageant and that I was out of it. I was happy, too, that Deacon Cass expected to get the rest of the money by the night of the show.

And I thought I knew somebody else who'd be joyful, too, at what had happened today. Mattywill would be tickled pink that I wouldn't be an angel. Well, let her be happy. Hopefully I wouldn't be in her way anymore by the time next spring rolled around.

We were home with the saddles in plenty of time for supper. At the table, Pa told everybody what had happened. Uncle Luke was surprised to hear that Abel and I were out of the pageant and wanted to know why.

"It's best for the sake of peace in Prineville," replied Pa.

"Now, Nate," said Uncle Luke, "I wouldn't do that. I wouldn't take 'em out."

"Luke, I don't like it, but people in town say our two families are 'hogging' the show. I want these people to come to my church next year. As it is now, they're angry because they were here before we Brants were, yet are excluded from the pageant. Besides, my children don't mind, do you, Bethany? Abel?"

I said, "I don't care."

Abel chimed in, "Me, neither, Pa. I been a shepherd before. And what I had to wear scratched me something awful."

Mattywill had kept quiet but spoke up now to ask, "But Billy Bob and I are still in it?"

Pa told her, "Yes, Mattywill, you both are still in it."

My cousin looked at me. I'd expected a big, happy, mean grin, but it wasn't there. There wasn't any expression on her face at all. She appeared to be thinking hard.

Pa went on to her, "I don't have any right to take you out of it, Mattywill. Nor do I want your folks to. You Morrises have been in this town a long time and should take part in your town's pageant. I've taken Bethany and Abel out. That's all."

"Billy Bob has to stay in because of all that ticket money?"

"Yes, that's right."

Mattywill nodded. "Uh-huh, that's fair where he's concerned."

And that was all my cousin said until Monday afternoon at school. I'd thought she'd tease me about my not being an angel, but she didn't say an unkind word to me.

When school was dismissed, she stopped by my desk and said, "Bethany, will you come up with me to see Miss Penny?"

Suspicious right off, I asked her, "Why? What're you up to, Mattywill Morris?"

"Something." Then she added, "Please come." As she said *please*, she smiled at me. It was like seeing the sun break through after a blizzard and it got me up out of my desk.

When I got to Miss Penny's desk with my cousin, Mattywill said, "Miss Penny, Bethany says her and Abel won't be in the Christmas pageant!"

"*She* and Abel, Mattywill. That is correct English and a correct statement as well."

"Bethany says, too, that you're gonna have a say about who fills their places?"

"I believe I may. What's on your mind, Mattywill?"

"Ma'am, I want to be out of it, too. If Bethany and Abel aren't in it, I don't want to be, either. Make one of the Macks a shepherd in my place."

I felt my jaw drop. I couldn't believe my ears.

Mattywill plowed on. "It ain't because I'm scared of the Macks. I can lick 'em any old time. It's because it's sort of true that we were hoggin' the pageant. This way only

Uncle Nate and Billy Bob are in it, so nobody can say we're big pigs anymore."

Miss Penny now did a strange thing. She rose up out of her desk, stuck out her right hand, and she and Mattywill shook hands just like men do. Miss Penny then said, "You're a brick, Mattywill. I'll let what you told me be known."

A brick? That was a new word for me. It didn't sound like a compliment, but if Miss Penny used it, then it had to be.

When Mattywill and I left, we walked out of the schoolhouse together and found Callie waiting for us. She'd hurried out past us, just as Miss Penny had finished talking. Outside, she grabbed hold of Mattywill and said, "You *are* a brick! That was just fine what you did in there. I heard it all. I'm gonna go back in and tell Miss Penny that I don't want to be a shepherd, either."

I caught Callie by the arm. "No, you stay in! You tell Arletta and Fairy Fay that we want them to have our parts. Tell 'em to go ask Mayor Cass for 'em today."

"I sure will, Bethany. But they won't be as good as you two."

"Heck sakes," came from Mattywill. "All I had to do was stand there and lean on a stick with a loop at the end. I'm supposed to admire my baby brother in the manger, but I see him all the time at home, remember?"

I let out a sigh of pure happiness. Queen Fareeta had fi-

132

nally been right about some good things coming my way. Everything was working out dandy for me now!

It went on being dandy. Arletta got the angel part, and Fairy Fay became Mattywill's shepherd. Abel's part was filled by his friend Jonadab. Miss Penny announced the changes at school the next day.

So everybody was happy. I heard that Mrs. Mack had even forgiven us for Billy Bob being the Baby Jesus now that her girls were to be an angel and a shepherd. Arletta brought us the news, along with big juicy pieces of fudge that Mrs. Mack made for Abel, Mattywill, and me. Arletta grinned as she gave them to us, saying, "Ma made fudge last night after I told her about the pageant. This is for you. Go ahead, you can eat it. It ain't poisoned."

As I ate it, I said, "Thank you, Arletta. You'll make a real fine angel. After you've practiced flying, be sure to tell me all about it. You won't ever forget it."

Even if we weren't in the pageant anymore, Mattywill, Abel, and I went to the second rehearsal of the show. I went to see how Arletta did. Aunt Reva stayed home with Billy Bob, who didn't have to come until the night of the pageant, December twenty-third. A big doll would take his place in Miss Penny's lap until then. After all, he didn't need to practice. All Billy Bob had to do was act natural.

That wasn't true of Arletta Mack. As we all craned our

necks, looking up, Arletta was dropped from the General Store balcony. She just stayed there twitching and jerking, and now and then going "oof." I knew just how she felt when Deacon Cass yelled at her to talk up and stop making noises—she was getting cut in two by the time the men started swinging her back and forth to fly.

When she was out of her harness, Arletta came over to Mattywill and me to sit down. She was holding her ribs the way I'd held mine the other Saturday. Panting, she told me, "Bethany, that's awful hard work!"

I nodded. "I know that, Arletta. I did it here, remember? I also did it where I used to live. The balcony they used there was even higher than this one. I got bruises on my ribs. Wait till you get your wings. Then you have to try to move those and talk, too. You know, they wanted me to blow a trumpet in Blue Fork, but thank goodness I didn't know how to play one. If I had, I wouldn't have had the wind to do it. You got to remember one more thing, too. You have to be careful you don't hit the Christmas star. They'll probably hang that down from the ceiling. It can get caught in your hair."

Arletta moaned, "Being an angel is exciting, but it's hard work."

"Being a preacher's kid is hard work, too," I said. "Preachers' kids hear all the time about being little angels."

Suddenly Arletta put a comforting hand on mine. "That must be hard to put up with."

"It is. Pa gets Abel and me into things we don't want to do sometimes."

Arletta told me, "I know. I wash the dishes more often than Fairy Fay does."

I shook my head. "I mean things harder than that."

"Like what?"

"Big chores that take time for us to do. Someday I'll tell you. Now I want to watch Callie and your sister and Jonadab marching to Bethlehem. They sure have to do a lot of walking back and forth to show how far it is."

After Arletta got up, rubbing her ribs, to sit beside her mother and twin brothers, Mattywill spoke softly to me. "Bethany, before you go, I got to tell you something. I need to. I'm sorry I was so mean-natured to you for so long."

I didn't look at her. I didn't say a word. After all, she *had* been mean-natured to me!

She asked, "Will you forgive me?"

"I guess so, but don't be mean to me again or I'll take it back. How come you changed toward me all of a sudden?"

"Because you gave up being an angel, and that job was just about the most exciting a girl could have. You didn't bawl or make any fuss about it, either. The angel's one of the most important parts of the show, and you gave it up. You were being noble, so I had to, too, even though I wasn't giving up anywhere near as much as you were. There are twelve shepherds and only one angel."

I had to sigh. "Oh, Mattywill, didn't you hear what Arletta said just now about being bruised about the midsection? I gave up flying, but I didn't give up much. Frog warts, don't give me anything I don't deserve."

"I like you now, Bethany. You helped me all summer with schoolwork, and I bet you didn't like doing that, either—not any more than I liked it."

I sighed some more. "To be truthful, I didn't. I did it to please your folks and my pa. It was all their idea. Can't grown-ups get kids into messes, though? I'm glad I did try to teach you, but I don't ever want to do it again. And while we're talking this way, I didn't like being on that elephant or being Miss Columbia afterward, either. All I wanted to do then was lie down somewhere for a spell and tremble all over with relief. That was one of the worst days of my life."

"I'm sorry. I didn't know. . . ."

She would have gone on, but the mayor shouted out, "Hush, all of you folks. Reverend Brant's about to read from the Good Book now that everybody's at the manger."

The night of the pageant, the poor shepherds sure had their hands full. Each shepherd had a live sheep to look after, and did they ever have trouble keeping the sheep out of the manger and the audience.

The cow and the donkey behind the Holy Family behaved just fine, and I couldn't see why the sheep hadn't been left out entirely; after all, the Bible said the shepherds "left their flocks." When I asked Uncle Luke about this during the show, he told me in a whisper that the sheep belonged to a man who wanted to show them off. So he paid Deacon Cass to get 'em in the pageant as prize livestock.

By the time the Wise Men had given their gifts to the Baby Jesus, every shepherd had a handful of sheep wool or was straddling a sheep or was kneeling and holding it tight around the neck. Pa had to yell Bible verses over the *baa* sounds because the sheep didn't like being held in and wanted to wander.

Arletta made a dandy angel on her ropes. She wore a long white gown with pantalettes. I noticed, though, that her muslin wings twitched more than they flapped when she moved her shoulders, but nobody seemed to notice. Nor did they see the one time the Star of Bethlehem hit her in the face. I saw her push it out of her way twice.

Miss Penny looked calm and beautiful in her blue robe, and Billy Bob just lay there in her lap, kicking and gurgling, not once spitting up on her. How proud we all were of him!

Everyone liked the pageant. There wasn't one hiss or boo during the whole thing. During the coffee and vinegar-pie social that followed the performance, Mayor Cass announced what the money tree and pot were for. As I ate my pie I watched folks flock around them to stick paper money into the tree with long pins, and I listened when a clank came from the pot. I couldn't tell how much was being pinned on and dropped in. A twenty-dollar gold piece would make just about the same amount of noise as a silver dollar did. And all the paper money I could see was just plain green.

So I was on needles and pins until late in the evening, waiting like all the others while Mayor Cass and his son took down the tree and carried off the pot to count the cash in the General Store owner's office.

How much was there? Would it be enough?

My heart climbed up to my mouth when Mayor Cass came out of the office. He held up his hands for quiet. Then he called out, "We did it, folks. My boy Deacon did it! We've got the money for the lumber for our church."

I looked at once to Pa's face. He was grinning. Then I watched him shake Uncle Luke by the hand and get a kiss on the cheek from Aunt Reva. Abel was jumping up and down and hugging Mattywill, who had thrown back her head laughing.

As for me, I shouted "Hurray" with everybody, and then after all the noise had quieted down, I called out, bold as brass, though my face was flaming red, "What about the minister's house?"

"There's enough for that, too."

When the others hurrayed again, I hurrayed as loud as I could.

Next Deacon Cass waved his arms to shut us all up so he could talk. "The labor to put up the church will be donated by the men here. After the turn of the year the lumber will come on the railroad. By spring the preacher and his family will be sitting pretty with a church and a house of their own. The lots they'll be built on are being donated, too—by Lawyer Templeton and Dr. Foxx."

After the turn of the year? That'd mean the lumber should be coming in January or February.

The turn of the year? The turn of the *century*!

1900 would see us home at last!

I went on staring at Deacon Cass as people crowded around him to shake his hand. He'd done the job, all right, I'd give him that, but I still didn't take to the way he did it. He made the hairs on the back of my neck prickle, and I had a strange hunch that we Brants weren't done with him yet.

THE TURN
OF THE
CENTURY

On the way home, tucked under old buffalo-skin robes in the wagon, Mattywill and I giggled a lot, cooking up a big surprise for our folks. To prove to everybody that our feuding and fussing was finally over, we came to the roast-beef Christmas Eve dinner hand in hand. Mattywill wore my red dress, and I wore her dark blue one.

This made Aunt Reva beam at us and say, "You two have just given me the best Christmas present I've ever had. Cousins ought to be loving."

Pa and Uncle Luke told us we looked pretty, and even Abel said, "Like I heard Pa say, they're old ladies' colors.

But they look better on you switched around. Please pass the gravy, Aunt Reva."

We didn't have a Christmas tree because there weren't any evergreens near Prineville, and we didn't hang up stockings, either. On Christmas morning we just got up and dressed, ate breakfast, and afterward exchanged presents. Mattywill and I gave our fathers matching mustache cups, and to her ma we gave a new bone crochet hook and a set of knitting needles. Together we gave Abel a harmonica and spinning top. Mattywill and I got identical gifts, taffeta hair bows of different colors, autograph albums, and silver-backed hairbrushes for the hundred licks a day Aunt Reva said girls ought to give their hair.

It was a dandy Christmas, that Christmas of 1899. Though there was some snow on the ground, all of us were snug in the warm house. Uncle Luke and Pa had gone out in wagons the day before to check on the cattle on the range and fetch them some hay to eat. They told us that the animals were all right and mighty glad to have their Christmas hay.

Christmas dinner was one I knew I'd always remember. It was stuffed roast goose. Aunt Reva had gotten up real early to render the grease out of it and then had cooked it all day long in a slow oven until the goose was the color of gold. With it we had potatoes and yams and vegetables she and I had canned last summer. There we all sat together—the three of us Brants and the four Morrises. Even Billy

Bob sat with us in his high chair for a little while. Everybody was there but Mama and our baby brother. I missed her so badly, my eyes misted, and while Uncle Luke blessed our food, I thought of Christmases in Blue Fork. Not last Christmas when Mama had been so sick and in bed while church ladies cooked our dinner, but happy ones when she'd been well. Mama had always made a lot out of Christmas. She knew all of the carols and holiday hymns. She decorated the church and manse with boughs so that they smelled piny-sweet inside. She made special cookies and paper chains with Abel and me and helped us paint nutshells with gold and silver paint to make our holiday table pretty.

During the second blessing, which Pa made after Uncle Luke, I wondered what Christmas 1900 would be like in our new manse. Would church ladies ask us to their families' dinners or would I have to cook it? Could I cook a goose? I doubted I could, though I had watched Aunt Reva carefully. Well, if I wasn't able to, we could all come out here to the ranch and share with our kinfolks. That gave me a warm feeling. They wouldn't desert us—ever.

Nobody came to call on us the way they used to in Blue Fork because the ranch was so far from town, but the cowboys in the bunkhouse got roast goose, too, from Aunt Reva. At night they came inside the house, sang carols, and drank a punch Uncle Luke made from home-preserved grape juice and whiskey. The cowboys surely took to it. It made them laugh and sing, and one of them fetched his guitar and played and sang us Mexican songs.

Pa didn't go to town that day to preach a sermon in the General Store. He had preached a holiday one the Sunday before, and it was mighty well received. Lots of folks had come up to him afterward to say that they would be coming to his church. I wished I'd heard him, but that Sunday had been my turn to stay home and tend to Billy Bob so Aunt Reva could go in to hear Pa. The Sunday before that, it'd been Mattywill's turn to watch the baby, and I'd gone. The time Pa spent circuit-riding sure gave him some good stories to tell in his sermons.

All of us went into Prineville the Saturday between Christmas and New Year's, riding to town in the old sleigh Uncle Luke brought out of the barn. Sleigh rides over the snow were fun, and I liked to hear the sound of the bells on the team's harness and watch the steam rising off the horses' backs.

Because it hadn't snowed for a couple of days, there'd been time for the streets of Prineville to get cleaned off. Strange, there were no horses in sight on the main street, but there were folks up on the boardwalk standing like they were waiting for something.

As Uncle Luke drove into town we were all wondering what was going on. I asked Mattywill, who was beside me in the back of the sleigh, "Is there going to be a parade? What day is it?"

"The twenty-eighth of December. Just three days to the new century. This day ain't a holiday that I know of."

143

"It *isn't* a holiday," I corrected her, knowing that she wanted me to now. "But something is going on. Look, there's Mayor Cass waving his hat."

And then we saw—or rather, we heard—why everybody was on the sidewalk and why all the horses were missing! Popping and thunking, hissing and bleating, it came toward us around the corner straight down Main Street like it was after us. It was a horseless carriage, the first one I'd ever set eyes on. Painted black and red, glittering with brass, it came bumping along, crossing from one side of the street to the other.

In spite of the goggles he wore and the big visored cap, I recognized the driver. Deacon Cass! Beside him, holding on to her broad-brimmed hat with one hand and to the side of the car with the other, sat Miss Penny.

As they came closer I saw that she wasn't grinning the way the mayor's son was. She was as white as candle wax.

"Good Lord!" exploded Pa. "Luke, tend to the horses!"

Oh, but Pa was right! Our team rose straight up in their traces, pawing the air. Their eyes rolling so that I could only see the whites, I knew that in another minute they'd bolt and run. The automobile really had spooked them.

Pa had sat up front with Uncle Luke and Aunt Reva, and now he was out of the sleigh like a shot. I never saw him move so fast. He ran to the team and grabbed hold of the bridle of the right-hand lead horse while it reared up over

144

him, its front legs flailing. If one of them hit him on the head, it could kill him.

I let out a squeak that was covered up by Pa's loud yell. "Turn off that confounded machine, you fool!" he shouted as he struggled with the horses.

Did Deacon Cass pay any heed to Pa? No, not he. Even though all of us screeched and screamed, he sailed right past our sleigh, his machine making loud nosies and evil smells while Pa clung to the bridle, being jerked up and down by the big nickering horse. Deacon even grinned and lifted his cap to Aunt Reva as he clattered by.

Beside me, I felt Abel turn to stare after the automobile. I kept my eyes on Pa, who was quieting down the right-hand horse while Uncle Luke sawed on the reins and talked to the team.

When the horses were quiet, though still trembling and jerking, Abel told me, "Miss Penny made him stop. He's still in the car, but she got out of it down the street. She's coming this way."

And so she was. Now that Pa was safe beside the calmed-down horses, I looked behind me and saw our teacher striding fast down the middle of the empty steet with everybody in Prineville staring at her. Deacon Cass sat alone in his horseless carriage, looking back over his shoulder at her.

She marched straight up to the sleigh. As she pinned her big black sailor hat more firmly to the top of her head, she said, "I am very sorry that this happened today. Everybody here in town knew that Mr. Cass was going to try out the new motorcar he just received. You didn't know that. I'm very sorry."

I had a horrible suspicion just then. Had he used our church and manse money? I asked Miss Penny.

"No, Bethany. His father bought it for him as a Christmas gift."

Now she turned to Pa and said, "That was very brave of you, Reverend Brant. I knew you were a fair man because of what you did about the Christmas pageant. Now I see you are also a man of courage."

"Why, thank you, Miss Penny!" came from Pa, who was smiling down at her.

I saw how she looked up at him. I thought it was admiring. Menfolk like to be admired. Mattywill and I had talked about how we'd both noticed that they lapped that up like cats lapped cream.

Miss Penny nodded. "I meant every word of it, Reverend. I trust you had a good Christmas?"

"Indeed we did," he told her.

"I am happy to hear it." She nodded to Aunt Reva, gave us a little wave of her hand, and turned around to go into the bonnet shop just across the way.

After she'd gone, more folks came up to tell Pa what a brave thing he'd done. I figured he had made some more friends for the church by doing it.

As for Deacon Cass, I thought he might have lost some. He didn't even get out of his machine to come back and say he was sorry. It seemed to me that he didn't much care if Pa or some of the rest of us might have gotten hurt. More than ever, I didn't take to that galoot. Maybe he'd raised the money for the church, and that was a good cause; but doing it hadn't made him a good man in my eyes.

Right then I heard popping sounds that told me the horseless carriage was starting up again. No, preacher's daughter or not, I wasn't full of Christmas kindness for Deacon Cass. He was too danged full of fondness for himself!

We all came in the sleigh to the New Year's Eve dance and soiree. The Dutchman was closed down as a saloon for the night and the soiree was held there, so finally I got to get a gander at the place. I'd been curious about the inside of a saloon for a long time. The big wooden floor was open for dancing, and chairs had been set along the walls for sitting. A long white-covered bar ran almost the length of one end of the saloon. It was piled with cooked hams and chickens, vinegar pies and fried pies, and chocolate cakes and drinks. For sure, we wouldn't start 1900 hungry! Opposite the bar was a platform with two fiddlers, a harmonica player, an accordion player, and a piano player on it.

On one side of the great big room were the menfolk, all duded up in suits or clean work clothes. The ladies sat in chairs on the other side. The richer ones were dolled up in taffeta and lace, the others wore calicoes and bombazine. Kids of all ages ran up and down in front of the rows of chairs having fun.

The dancing had just started as we got there. While I held Billy Bob, Uncle Luke led Aunt Reva out onto the floor in a waltz. Abel left us to run up and down with Jonadab, and Mattywill went to stand giggling with Arletta, Callie, and Fairy Fay, her friends now, too. Pa sat down beside me to listen to the music.

I said to him, "Look at that old Deacon Cass over there dressed in black and wearing a tailcoat and a boiled shirt."

"Now, Bethany, I wear black and white, too."

"You come by it honest, Pa, as a reverend. He isn't a real deacon. He's just duded up."

"Maybe he'll be a real deacon someday."

I snorted. "As bad as he is, always scheming, not caring about other folks? If he comes to our church, you've got your work cut out for you, Pa."

This made Pa chuckle. He said, "Maybe so. Maybe so."

Just then Miss Penny came into the saloon. I watched Deacon hurry over to help her off with her coat. She looked real pretty tonight in a pale yellow georgette gown with a cream-colored lace bertha and stand-up collar. Yellow suited her just fine. It made her look good enough to eat.

I watched Cass swing her out into a polka and whirl her around and around. Everybody was looking and admiring them. They went on dancing together, dance after dance—

waltzes, more polkas, schottisches, square dances, and the Varsouvienne, like they'd never get weary.

I'd worked up an appetite minding Billy Bob, and after Aunt Reva returned, I went to the buffet bar and filled a tiny plate with some grub.

Callie joined me and we ate together. She looked very nice tonight. Her hair was combed out pretty well, and she wore a bright green plaid dress somebody had given her. As we ate, she told me, "Bethany, the Ladies' Choice Dance is coming up pretty soon. I seen 'em happen before. Generally it's a galoot who asks a lady, but this time it's her turn to ask him. I think that's only fair, don't you? Why should the men do all the asking and the ladies do all the sitting around in chairs?"

I thought about that. No, it wasn't fair. It should be fifty-fifty when it came to asking. I said, "Maybe ladies would say no to galoots they don't like the looks of."

"No, they can't do that, Bethany. That's just about the rudest thing a lady can do to a man, outside of shooting him."

"You mean when we're grown-up and get asked to dance, we have to dance with everybody who asks us?"

"That's what I been told."

"That's terrible, Callie!"

"I think so, too."

Callie would have said more, but suddenly the music stopped.

The accordion player got up and called out, "The next

set of six pieces is a Ladies' Choice. Ladies, you go to one side of the room. When we start up again, run and get your galoot."

What a lot of laughing there was from the women while the men stood, trying to look like they didn't care if they got asked or not.

I saw Aunt Reva and Mrs. Mack stay with their babies, but a lot of ladies came sailing forward to the gents. Miss Penny was one of them in the lead. I kept my eyes on her real good. She came straight toward Deacon Cass, who had begun to grin. But all at once she turned around and went back, sashaying down the line of seated ladies, passing them, heading for chairs at the very end.

That's where Uncle Luke and Pa were sitting.

I held my breath.

Smiling, my schoolteacher went up to Uncle Luke and held out her hand. But he was a married man!

No, her hand wasn't held out to him, after all, but to Pa. Frog warts!

Miss Penny had picked my father for the Ladies' Choice, while half the jaspers in town had been brushing the sides of their hair or twisting their mustaches or straightening their neckties, hoping she'd pick them. She'd picked Pa over all of them and over Deacon Cass, too!

What would he do? Would he, a preacher, dance? He was still wearing a mourning arm band for Mama. Would it be respectable for him to dance? Did he even know how?

◄§ 12 §►

NOT THE JASPER
I WAS
EXPECTING!

Well, did I ever get a surprise!

Pa got up, took Miss Penny's hand, put his arm around her waist, and off they went into a dance. I'd never once seen Pa dance with Mama, but he sure did know how. I figured it must be like learning to swim—something you never did forget.

I looked all around me fast, to see if people were whispering because the minister was dancing. But, nobody seemed to be paying him or Miss Penny any heed except for me.

No, I was wrong. There was another one. Deacon Cass! His eyes were popping out of his face, which had gone all red. He'd expected Miss Penny to choose him and she hadn't. I heard a man next to him laugh out loud and saw grins on the faces of some other men. No lady had asked him. Oh, was his nose out of joint! He grabbed two glasses of punch off the bar and tossed down both of them fast. Then he turned around and went out through the swinging doors, moving so fast that he swept them wide apart.

I looked on while Pa finished the first dance of the set with my teacher, then led the way to two empty chairs a distance from Uncle Luke and Aunt Reva. He'd danced one dance to be polite, but he'd sit the other ones out the way a reverend in mourning should. I was proud of Pa for knowing what to do. I figured he planned to sit out the next five pieces with Miss Penny, talking to her.

Just then Abel came running up to me, panting hard and sliding over the polished floor like the devil was at his heels.

He cried at me, "Did you see Pa dancing?"

"I sure did, Abel. I didn't know he could."

Abel sniffled. As I wiped his nose with my handkerchief I told him, "Deacon Cass was expecting Miss Penny to ask him, but she picked Pa."

Abel nodded. "Deacon Cass has got a lot of punch in him. But it's full of brandy likker even if it don't taste like it. Jonadab told me that his and Callie's pa put the brandy in. I heard Cass tell another galoot that he changed all the money collected for the church and manse into paper money and he's got it on him right now."

"All our money with *him* right now?" I was horrified.

"That's right. Right after midnight, 1900, he's gonna

give it to his pa with everybody lookin' on, and his pa will tell the folks that it's ready to go to the new bank safe across the street. The banker'll put it in his safe, and anybody who wants to is welcome to come along and watch it. The sheriff'll be guarding it."

Abel kept talking; but all I could think of was that Deacon Cass had all the money on him! I looked around wildly, and the first thing I saw was the sheriff talking with the mayor.

Then I looked at the saloon's double doors. I told my brother, "Abel, for heaven's sake, go round up Callie and Arletta and Fairy Fay and Jonadab and any other kids you trust. We can't let Deacon Cass out of our sight. And he's out of it right now. He just went outside. He's got all of our money on him. Robbers might get him. How many folks heard him talking about the money?"

"He was loud in the mouth. A whole bunch of 'em did, Bethany."

"Abel, run and fetch the other kids. Hurry up."

"Shall we tell Pa and Uncle Luke?"

"We don't want to take the time to explain. Besides, the kids'll know Prineville better'n Uncle Luke and Pa do. They're town kids, aren't they? Don't pick any who aren't. Just tell 'em we *have* to find Deacon Cass fast!"

"Sure, sis."

My mind racing like a spooked horse, I watched Abel gather the Mack girls and boys and Callie, Mattywill, Jonadab, and some of our other classmates. What if somebody had already knocked Deacon on the skull and gotten the church money? I prayed it would be all right. Oh, how I prayed for him.

When everyone was together, I told them, as fast as I could, what was going on. At the end I said, "We just have to find him! Go in pairs. If you find him, one of you keep an eye on him and the other one run back and tell me where he is."

Fairy Fay said, "Bethany, it's cold outside. My coat's buried deep under other ones on the table."

"Fairy Fay Mack, this is more important than a couple of shivers or sneezes. Hurry up. Mattywill, you stay here with me."

"I planned to," said my cousin.

I glanced over now to where Pa and Miss Penny had been sitting. They were gone. That had been fast. I looked wildly over the saloon but couldn't see hide nor hair of them. Where were they? They must have gone outside to get some fresh air. Aunt Reva and Uncle Luke were gone, too, but I knew they were going to go. They'd said they intended to leave around eleven o'clock to go visit an old friend who was sick. They wanted to show him Billy Bob. He'd been too ill to see the baby before. They planned to see in 1900 with their old friend.

Should I run to Mayor Cass and tell him about his son? No, he was out on the dance floor now, hopping around with a fat lady who must have asked him late in the Ladies' Choice to schottische with her.

"Oh, Mattywill," I wailed. "We're the only ones here in our time of trouble."

Had I done wrong in not going to Pa right away? Would he be mad at me if Deacon Cass got robbed?

"Oh, Mattywill," I wailed again.

She put her arm around my waist and let me lean on her shoulder. "Don't fret, Bethany. The kids'll find him. If he fell down drunk or crawled under the boardwalk, they'll roust him out. I saw him leave, too. It wasn't long ago at all. He can't have gone very far."

"But he could have run into robbers just outside the saloon doors!"

"Don't think about it. We just got to wait, Bethany."

So while folks ate and drank and danced all around us, not noticing anything at all, we waited and fretted. It taught me a lesson. You could sure feel bad in a happy crowd.

Suddenly the saloon doors opened on one side, and a Mack twin, the one who'd paired off with Callie, came running in, pushing past the dancers up to Mattywill and me.

He panted to us, "We got the galoot—Callie Stark and me. Callie's keeping watch on him."

"Where is he? What's he doing? Is he dead?"

"No." The boy pointed to the ceiling. "He's up there— over the saloon."

"What's he doing up there?"

"Playing cards."

Lord, give me strength, I prayed! Cards? Poker? *The church money!*

Running, the three of us left the Dutchman. We streaked across the front porch, leapt down off it into the snow, and ran to the outside stairs through a shoveled-off path. With me in the lead we pounded up the steps and stopped at the very top where Callie stood waiting for us.

I asked her, "Is he playing cards?"

"Look for yourself, Bethany."

I peered through the glass set in the door, and my heart fell down into my best boots. There sat a red-faced Deacon Cass at a round table with four other men. Yes, he was playing cards. I knew enough to know that five cards in a man's hand probably meant a poker game, and there were five cards lying facedown in front of Deacon next to a couple of hundred-dollar bills. In the center of the table was a pile of gold and silver coins and more paper money. The pot!

As I watched with my hair standing on end, I saw a man across from Cass ask him something. I couldn't hear what he was saying.

The mayor's son didn't answer him. All at once he pitched forward on his face next to his spread-out cards. He'd passed out!

What could I do? What should I do? I had to do something.

So I opened the door and went inside. Mattywill, Callie, and the little Mack boy followed me in.

The first thing I heard was a growl from one of the men. "No kids allowed in here. Go back downstairs to the party."

"Go away, you brats," said another man.

I hated being called that. Angry now, I told them all, "No, we won't! That money Deacon Cass is playing cards with is money collected to build my father, the new minister, a church and us a house to live in. Give it back to me right now and I'll leave."

Callie spoke up. "It's three thousand dollars."

The black-bearded man who'd spoken first to us said, "We can't do that, little sister. This is a poker game and we got rules to follow."

A bald-headed man who hadn't spoken until now told me, "Go get somebody growed-up from your church to play young Cass's hand. He claimed it was a good one. Get your pa to come up here and play it for Cass."

Pa? Play cards? No, he might have danced, but he wouldn't touch cards.

I said, "Pa's a preacher. He doesn't hold with cards."

"That's too bad," came from the first man. "Well, boys, what'll we do?"

The bald jasper said, "Jace, we could leave the pot right where it is, pick up Cass's cards, shuffle 'em into the deck, and let the whole shebang go to whoever gets the highest card out of the deck—one of the kids or one of us. It'd be an interestin' way to end up 1899."

I asked, "The whole shebang?" motioning toward the pot of coins and paper.

"That's right, little lady. There's over five thousand dollars in it."

So I was a little lady now, was I? Things had moved too fast to suit me. I looked to Mattywill and Callie. After a while they nodded their heads. They thought we ought to play for the highest card in the deck.

I asked, "What do I do? Which one of us should do it?"

The black-bearded man, Jace, growled. "We'll choose the kid. Which one of you is the oldest here? Let her do it."

Oh, no. Me! I said weakly, "That's me. I'm the oldest one."

"Then it'll be *you* who plays for the church folks."

"I can't!" I told them.

"You got to," Mattywill whispered to me.

I nodded, weak as a kitten, feeling the sweat come out of my forehead.

"Wait a minute," cried Callie. "If Bethany plays for the church, I shuffle the cards."

"Don't you trust us, honey?" asked the fourth man.

"Not much. My pa used to be a gambler." Callie smiled in spite of her paleness. She went on. "I'm just a kid, so you can be sure I won't cheat when I shuffle." Saying this, she picked up Deacon Cass's cards and held out her hand for the others to give her theirs.

Once she had them all, she sat down in the empty chair beside Deacon Cass, who was snoring, shuffled once, and again, then spread out the whole deck of cards across the top of the table.

The bald-headed galoot said, "The yellow-headed gal draws last."

We watched each man draw one card, slowly pulling it from the fanned-out deck. One man's hand hovered over the cards, moving this way and that until he snaked out one card. The others picked theirs faster.

In a few seconds it was my turn. What should I do? Stand back because I was a preacher's daughter and ask Mattywill who was my kin to draw instead of me? She would if I asked her. No, that wouldn't be right. That would put the card-playing sin on both of us—me for asking and her for doing.

Oh, what a pickle I was in now! More bad stuff, as Queen Farcetu had said. For anyone else but a preacher's daughter this decision wouldn't have been half so hard. But I had a lot to live up to—more than any other kids I knew. Abel and I hadn't asked to be born into a minister's family. Mama had known what she was getting into when she married a preacher, but we didn't have a choice.

Besides, she was naturally good. I wasn't—not naturally. I had to work hard for it. I didn't always like Pa volunteering me to do good deeds, and I didn't like doing them just because he wanted me to. If I did one, I wanted it to be because the idea of doing it had come out of my own head, not somebody else's—not even his. He'd gotten a "call" to be a preacher. Well, for quite a spell I'd been getting a "call" to be myself, Bethany Clarinda Brant. I wanted to be the way *I* wanted to be—to behave like myself first, not always to be a preacher's daughter first!

I made up my mind. It was my turn now, and *I'd draw*! I leaned over the cards, wondering which one to pick. I looked at each man in turn. Two were grinning at me. They must have gotten high cards.

As I muttered a prayer, asking in my mind for Mama's advice, it was as if she'd spoken to me in my head, saying, "Take the right card, Bethany."

What did that mean? Be sure to draw a high card or take the card at the very right end of the row?

I took a deep breath, and then I pulled out the card that was farthest to the right at the very end. Carefully I slid it along the table and brought it up to my chest. Still praying, I looked at it.

The man on the card had a little beard. He didn't have a crown on his head, so I knew that what I'd drawn wasn't a king. From hearing folks talking about cards, I knew it had to be a jack. From the red heart-shaped things on the sides I figured out that I'd drawn a jack of hearts. He was looking straight ahead, the side of his face to me.

Jace ordered slowly, "All right, let's lay down our cards and turn 'em faceup."

He turned up a black ten. Even if he'd grinned at me, I saw that I'd beaten him, at least. Three more to go!

The galoot on his right turned up a red three. Two more to go!

The man to the right of him had a red seven, a seven of hearts. Just one more to go.

The last man had been a grinner, and I was scared. I held my breath. This last jasper, the bald one, turned up his card. It was another jack, a black one.

A *second* jack? I felt like fainting. Would we have to draw all over again?

"What's yours, girlie?" asked the bald man.

Shaking by now, I put down my jack faceup, wishing it had been an ace or king or queen.

"She drew a one-eyed jack! A cussed one-eyed jack!" said the bald gambler in disgust.

A one-eyed jack? *A one-eyed man!* Why, of course, he was one-eyed. I could only see his profile, and that had only one eye.

Queen Fareeta had struck once more! I'd met my one-eyed man, after all.

Callie cried out, *"Bethany wins! A jack of hearts is higher than a jack of clubs. Take the money, Bethany."*

I looked at the pile of coins and paper money. Over five thousand dollars. I'd never seen so much money before in all my life. That was lots more than was needed for our church and manse. There was maybe money here to buy a steeple, stained-glass windows, an organ, and a church bell. What a church we'd have if I took it all! After all, I *had* won it with the help of my one-eyed jack.

No, I couldn't take it all. I fought down temptation. I told Callie, "Take only the three thousand dollars that was collected for the church and manse. No more. Let 'em have the rest of the danged pot!"

I nodded to the men. "Happy New Year to you all.

Please mend your ways in the new century. That's what Pa would tell you. He'd be pleased to see you come to our church. You need it."

And so out we went with the money, leaving Deacon Cass to sleep it off. As we went down the stairs we heard pistol shooting and shouting from below.

It was the New Year coming in. It was 1900! The twentieth century was upon us!

We found Pa and Miss Penny standing out in the street in the snow, looking up at the beautiful, clear night sky. Folks ran around them, shooting off pistols, yelling and kissing each other.

Pa wasn't paying any heed to that. He was pointing out the constellations in the winter sky to Miss Penny. He was good at astronomy.

The mayor and the banker were standing on the saloon porch. Mayor Cass, I noticed, seemed to be looking this way and that way in the crowd. I guessed he was looking for his son and the money.

Well, we had the money now. I marched up to them all, and I told the mayor, "If you're looking for your boy, he's passed out drunk upstairs. He took it real hard when Miss Penny didn't pick him in the Ladies' Choice dances. Before he went upstairs, though, he gave us the church money so he wouldn't lose it in a poker game."

To spare the mayor's feelings I'd told a white lie. I didn't truly have any bad nature toward him. He'd been nice to

me when he made me the Gem of the Ocean. Telling him
the truth now would be a mean thing and would make him
feel sad on New Year's Eve.

The mayor looked astonished. "Deacon gave it to *you
kids?*"

"Sure," I said, still white-lying. "I'm the preacher's oldest kid. Deacon knew we wouldn't gamble it away."

I told myself young Cass would be too drunk to remember what had really happened, and I was sure he'd never
seen us in the upstairs room. Maybe the other men there
would tell him what went on—maybe not. Anyhow, his pa,
a man I liked, didn't need to know the whole wicked truth.

As we emptied our pockets into the cloth money bag the
banker had ready, Mattywill told him, "Mister, every red
cent's there. I know. I'm a good arithmeticker."

He smiled. "I bet you are, my dear."

Even though Abel had already told me, I just couldn't
help but ask the mayor, "How come the money wasn't put
in the bank right after the Christmas pageant? How come
your son had it on him?"

He nodded at me. "For a child that is an intelligent question, indeed. Deacon had to change the money into paper to
make it light enough to carry. He did the collecting, remember? He wanted to make a big splash tonight when we
gave the money to Banker Burnett here. Too bad my boy
missed it. I'll have some stern words with him later."

Being trained to find the good in folks—to hunt hard for

it sometimes—I decided there was one thing to be said for Deacon Cass. He could like a lady well enough to have to drown his sorrows if she didn't like him. That meant he had a heart, even if he didn't show much brain. So there was hope for him to turn out to be a good man. I was tempted to tell his pa that, too, but kept it to myself as the kindly thing to do. His pa would deal with him for sure, and I was pretty sure he was done for with Miss Penny, to boot.

Now the mayor called for everybody to "gather around" because he and the banker were going to put the church fund into the safe.

The other kids were back from their hunting by now, and we all went along to watch. After all the trouble we went through for this money, we were going to see it safely stashed away!

The metal safe was big and black, and it sort of squatted in a back corner of the bank. The banker inserted a heavy key into the lock, and when the thick door was open, I crowded closer with Mattywill beside me. The banker shoved the cloth bag into the safe; then, with a bang, he shut the door, locked it up again, and put the key into his breast pocket.

As he straightened up he caught my eye. He grinned and asked, "Are you satisfied that the money's safe in my safe, Miss Columbia, the Gem of the Ocean?"

"Yes, sir, I am. We all saw with our own eyes where it is, and that's good enough for all of us."

Mattywill added, "Just don't loan it out to anybody."

"You may rest easy on that score. It's earmarked for the church. Now let's go back and celebrate the New Year."

As we ate cold fried chicken and boiled eggs back at the Dutchman Saloon, Callie whispered into my ear, "Bethany, your pa's been outside a long time with Miss Penny. They're still out there in the cold. I saw her choose him to dance with. I bet she's sort of sweet on him." She laughed. "How'd you like a schoolmarm for a stepmama?"

I sighed. "Callie Stark, there's many a slip twixt the cup and the lip. Mama hasn't been gone a year yet, and Pa loved her dearly. Maybe Miss Penny's setting her cap for him, maybe not. I like her. But Pa won't rush into things."

Callie said apologetically, "I didn't mean any harm. Why are you frowning so?"

"Because I just have to have a talk with Pa real soon, and it won't be about my playing cards tonight. That'll be our secret for a while, I think. I'll tell him later on. Will you keep it secret?"

"Sure," said Callie, then Mattywill, then the Mack boy. "Will you talk about Miss Penny?" Callie asked next.

"No, about something else."

"What'd that be?"

"About behaving myself so much of the time. It's wearing down my nerves. Look at how I sweated when I had to draw that card. It wasn't just because I was nervous and scared. It was also because doing that wasn't something a preacher's daughter ever ought to have done. It was gambling. I couldn't rightly ask one of you to do it, because I truly was the oldest. And I couldn't ask you to do my dirty work because that would have been wicked of me. No matter how I looked at it, I'd be doing something bad. But because it was for our church and we'd worked hard for it, I just had to do it. And I did it! It isn't easy to be good all the time unless it comes natural, and it isn't natural to me the way it is to Pa." I turned and looked Callie full in the face. "You aren't kin to a reverend. You just don't know what I mean—what I go through all the time. Mattywill does a little bit, though."

"I surely do. It's no picnic being a preacher's kid." Mattywill laughed and said, "If Miss Penny ever does get hitched to your pa, Bethany, you'd better tell her what she's in for. It'd be your duty."

"Mattywill, if anybody knows what her duty is, it's a preacher's daughter!" I lifted my glass of pink lemonade. "Here's to 1900! Thanks to my good friends here, we've got a church, and soon we Brants will have a roof over our heads. Happy New Year, everybody!"

AUTHOR'S NOTE

In this novel I have written of a number of things that will be unfamiliar to today's young readers.

Sad but true, the deaths of both mother and newborn infant in childbirth were not rarities in the last century, though they are almost unheard of today with full-term babies. Twentieth-century medicine has made great progress in the care of mothers-to-be and their unborn infants. Diseases that killed many people in the nineteenth century have either been stamped out or can now be controlled by very effective methods.

I have written here about preachers who were circuit riders in the Western states. Some preached until they got a church building. Others spent years doing this because they felt "called" to it. In Texas, circuit riders were called "cowboy preachers." Sometimes they rode horseback ninety miles at a stretch to reach the next ranch or town and marry, bury, and baptize. Often they held prayer meetings in groves beside creeks and rivers. Settlers would come to week-long camp meetings by wagon from fifty miles around, and families built their own huts to live in. These preachers sometimes found danger on the way not only from flooded rivers, tornadoes and other storms, and wild animals, but also from outlaws and renegade Indians who wanted the minister's horse, saddle, and scanty supplies. In the early twentieth century some circuit-riding ministers (they were mostly Roman Catholic, Presbyterian, Baptist, and Church of Christ) used automobiles to travel the flatter parts of the West. However, some routes were not passable by means other than horseback, even into the era of the 1930s. (Judges were also circuit riders in frontier times and faced the same perils preachers did.)

Frontier community churches were often subscribed for—the towns collected money to erect them. Generally the chief men of the town did this, though anyone connected with the church-to-be could help, from the minister on down to the Sunday school children. Until a church was built, services could be held anywhere, even in saloons, or outdoors, wherever there was some shelter from the weather.

Teachers were very poorly paid in the old West. Being

given food and a room by a family was counted part of the teacher's pay. Besides, the teacher was considered very, very respectable, so she could not be expected to live in a hotel or boardinghouse where single men also lived. Had she done so, she might be gossiped about, and that could cost her her job. Rotating with families as a guest could not always have been pleasant. Imagine the twitchiness of a teacher who would see her pupils twenty-four hours a day while living in their home. On the other hand, her students must have felt constantly under her critical, correcting gaze.

The McGuffey readers were famous school texts of the last century and this. Famed educator William Holmes McGuffey, born in America in 1800, compiled them, and by 1900 they were in use in thirty-seven states. Illustrated, moral in tone, broad in culture, they combined carefully selected literary prose pieces from noted nineteenth-century British and American authors and poetry from such as Byron and Longfellow. The readers sold over one hundred twenty million copies between 1836 and 1920 in their several revisions. (As of 1978 they sold thirty thousand copies a year—probably more as nostalgic mementoes than actual school readers.) It is hard to overestimate the influence of McGuffey's work. Generations of young Americans had their thinking shaped by his readers. Education past grade school was often beyond the reach of most children as being too expensive (high schools charged tuition in many places) or too far distant. What thousands of Americans learned about literature and poetry came only from their exposure to McGuffey readers.

Bethany and Mattywill's argument in my book is actually drawn from the fourth McGuffey reader, which features two selections from Daniel Defoe's *Robinson Crusoe* and also a nature study piece on elephants using the word "proboscis" for snout or trunk or nose!

In this book I've given a lot of space to a Christmas pageant. Children's pageants in churches were a big feature of nineteenth-century America. They were an excellent dramatic way to teach Bible stories about Easter and the Nativity and to educate the often illiterate adults and children. Pageants added color to lives that could be drab and hard for adults. Our ancestors took them seriously, though they were homespun affairs with nothing of the slickness of today's television productions. Of course, humorous things sometimes took place at Christmas pageants as they naturally would when excited children and startled animals were brought together, but the inadvertent humor didn't interfere long with the sacredness of the occasion.

I've also written of prefabricated houses, which must seem a very modern concept. They certainly are not. Schools and churches, as well as stores and residences, were purchased by catalog model and number. They could run in price from several hundred dollars to two or three thousand, depending on size and fanciness. The sawed-to-size lumber was shipped by boat or railroad to the buyer and erected on his land, according to the directions that came with the lumber. Today the prices of such buildings seem laughable, but at the turn of the century the dollar purchased much, much more than it does nowadays. A factory worker was well paid at $7 per week or nearly $30 per month. A man's long-wearing work shirt could be bought for 38 cents, a solid gold pocket watch for $14, a fine oak rocking chair for $3.75, and a sofa for $15. It is an interesting fact that some old prefab houses are sought after today for residences because they were so well constructed.

The very words *preacher's son* evoke the image of a boy who behaves badly, a "hell-raiser" who rebels against religion. They are stock figures in American folklore, as are ministers' wives and daughers, who are often portrayed as rather self-effacing, colorless, long-suffering women.

Life could be hard for nineteenth-century women. Poor women, married or unmarried, worked long hours with their hands as seamstresses, mill workers, and laundresses. Better educated women could be schoolteachers as long as they remained unmarried. In most communities, when they got married, they had to stop teaching. The vast majority of women then stayed home and kept house because it was the "proper" thing for women to do. They took no part in their husband's, brother's, or father's businesses. There were almost no women doctors or lawyers, and surely no firefighters, jockeys, or bankers. They rarely handled the family finances. Men did that. They could not vote. Men did that. They could not expect to have their opinions considered valuable. Any woman who tried to do something in the arts or in the business world was looked at with righteous shock and could be denied the society of "good women." Most women "behaved"—not to anger the men in their lives. It is to be hoped that my Bethany Brant would find her father willing to permit her her freedom of expression. (I have depicted him as an unusually sensitive man. I suspect he would listen to her grievances with understanding!)

—Patricia Beatty
June 1985